Seoul's Historic *Walks*

Second Edition

Seoul's Historic Walks
Second Edition

Written by Cho In-Souk & Robert Koehler
Map Illustration by Hwang Kwang-hee

Copyright © 2008, 2009 by Seoul Foundation for Arts and Culture

Seoul Foundation for Arts and Culture
517 Cheonggyecheonno Dongdaemun-gu, Seoul 130-823, Korea
Phone (82-2) 3290-7000
http://www.sfac.or.kr

First published in 2008 by **Seoul Selection**
105-2 Sagan-dong, Jongno-gu, Seoul, 110-190, Korea
Phone (82-2) 734-9567, Fax (82-2) 734-9562
http://www.seoulselection.com
Email: publisher@seoulselection.com

ISBN: 978-89-91913-31-8
Printed in the Republic of Korea

This book is produced under the sponsorship of
Seoul Foundation for Arts & Culture

Contents

When Sunday comes,
My friend
When shall we look for the last
Alleyway which we have missed and not yet visited
With our eyes wide open?
.....
Shall we visit even an alleyway
we have not yet visited?
.....
Now shall we look for the last
Alleyway which we have missed and not yet visited
With our eyes wide open?

The above are a few lines from a poem from the famous Korean lyrical poet "Midang" Seo Jeong-ju.

On the fourth Sunday of the month, the Seoul Foundation for Arts and Culture looks through the streets of Seoul in search of the city's hidden cultural resources.

This book is the result. It ties together the tales of Seoul not often seen in most tourist books. I'm sure that foreigners will be able to conduct fun and intellectually interesting tours using this book. If you walk the paths suggested by this book, you may create wonderful unexpected memories.

Ahn Ho-sang

CEO, Seoul Foundation for Arts and Culture

Second Edition Preface

Since its first release in March 2008, *Seoul's Historic Walks* has received the constant appreciation of readers. It seems that tourists visiting Seoul and resident foreigners like the book because it's easy to carry and introduces Seoul's historic spots with interesting stories. We are happy to release this second edition only after a year and a half.

The origin of *Seoul's Historic Walks* goes back to 1991 when Daaree Architect & Associates initiated a program called "Finding Seoul." Its goal was to allow participants an opportunity to experience—on foot—the architecture in which we live our lives and the structure and history of this city we call Seoul. The program featured expert lectures, on-site tours and debates. It met with unexpected success.

From March to May 2001, I conducted the "Exploring Seoul" program for members of the Seoul International Women's Association. This program was started to introduce—from an expert point of view—a side of Seoul perhaps unknown to the city's foreign residents.

When, in 2007, I was entrusted to handle the "Culture is My Friend" walking tour program for the Seoul Foundation for Arts and Culture (SFAC), I developed eight three-hour tours divided by theme. The 2008 tour included the recently restored Geoncheonggung Royal Residence in Gyeongbokgung Palace, so we've included a section on 19th century royal residence architecture in this revised edition. We've also corrected a few minor errors that made their way into the first edition.

I held my last SFAC walking tour in 2008. What we learned in those tours remains in this book, however, so I hope that knowledge will be passed on to people who wish to learn about Seoul. I'd also like to thank Seoul Selection for their hard work in putting this book together, and above all, I thank the SFAC for making this volume possible.

Cho In-Souk, August 2009

Seoul is a city best discovered on foot.

A world-class city of 11 million people, Seoul is a place where tradition and modernity exist side-by-side, often in jarring contrast. But to truly appreciate the city's rich history, you need to get off the tourist path and do a bit of walking.

Seoul is much more than just the major tourist spots like Gyeongbokgung Palace and Insa-dong. Whether it's hiking along Seoul Fortress high in the mountains overlooking downtown or strolling through the quaint alleyways of Bukchon, there's always something to discover as long as you're willing to do the exploring. In the city's hidden alleyways and remote hillsides, you can experience first-hand the dramatic transformation of a city from walled medieval town to dynamic 21st century metropolis, all in little more than a century.

This book will guide you along the walks conducted by the Seoul Foundation for Arts and Culture during its "Culture Is My Friend" program of 2007–2008. These walks, conducted in Korean and English every last Sunday of the month from March to September, gave Seoul residents—both Korean and foreign—an opportunity to learn about Seoul's history and development as they were guided through the city's historic streets and alleys. This guidebook is a humble effort to give solo walkers the opportunity to experience the wonder and beauty of "hidden" Seoul at their own leisure.

A word of warning, however. This guidebook is not meant to be exhaustive. As you make your way through the walks introduced here, you'll no doubt come across places deserving of mention in these pages. The key here is to explore. Don't be confined by what you read here; let your legs be your guide.

The Heart of Historic Seoul

TOUR* 1
The Heart of Historic Seoul

Sungnyemun Gate to Gwanghwamun Gate

Today, Seoul is a vast metropolitan region spanning both sides of the Hangang River and serviced by a complex system of subways, buses and commuter trains. This was not always so, however. For centuries, Seoul—the royal capital of the Joseon kingdom—was a walled city surrounded by the Hangang River to the south and mountains to the north, east and west.

This walk will take us through the heart of old Seoul, from the iconic Sungnyemun Gate in the south to the Gyeongbokgung Palace in the north. Along the way, we'll be able to experience Korea's development from a medieval walled city into the modern metropolis that it is today.

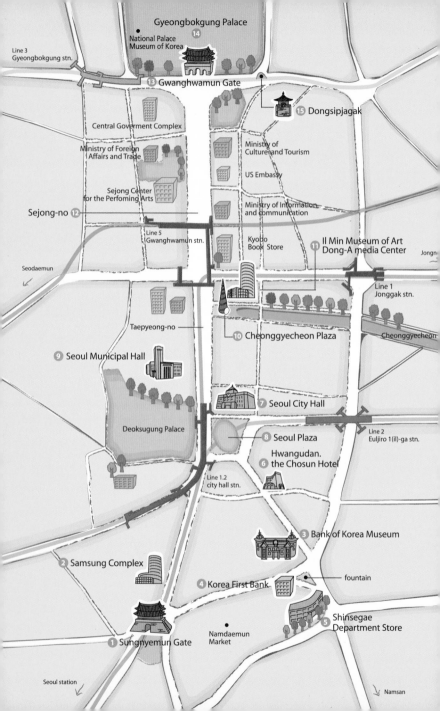

Gyeongbokgung Palace

14

National Palace
Museum of Korea

Line 3
Gyeongbokgung stn.

13 Gwanghwamun Gate

Central Goverment Complex

15 Dongsipjagak

Ministry of Foreign
Affairs and Trade

Ministry of
Culture and Tourism

US Embassy

Sejong Center
for the Perfoming Arts

Ministry of Information
and communication

Sejong-no **12**

Line 5
Gwanghwamun stn.

Kyobo
Book Store

Il Min Museum of Art
Dong-A media Center **11**

Jongn

Seodaemun

Line 1
Jonggak stn.

Taepyeong-no

10 Cheonggyecheon Plaza

Cheonggyecheon

9 Seoul Municipal Hall

7 Seoul City Hall

Deoksugung Palace

Line 2
Euljiro 1(il)-ga stn.

8 Seoul Plaza

Hwangudan.
6 the Chosun Hotel

Line 1.2
city hall stn.

3 Bank of Korea Museum

2 Samsung Complex

fountain

4 Korea First Bank

5 Shinsegae
Department Store

1 Sungnyemun Gate

Namdaemun
Market

Seoul station

Namsan

1 ❋ Sungnyemun Gate

Arguably Korea's most famous national landmark, **Sungnyemun Gate**—the principal gate of old Seoul's surrounding fortress walls—served for centuries as the southern gateway to the royal capital. It is also known as Namdaemun ("Great South Gate") due to its location. Before a devastating fire in 2008, the imposing gate, with its magnificent Korean-style roof, was the oldest wooden structure in Seoul. Urban development over the last century has led to the city spilling out beyond the old city walls, but Sungnyemun still marks the beginning of the historic city center. Due to its historic and architectural value, it has been designated Korea's National Treasure No. 1.

Sungnyemun once stood isolated on a traffic island amidst one of Seoul's busiest roads. One British newspaper even referred to the gate as "Asia's most dangerous tourist attraction." Several years ago, however, a grassy plaza was constructed around the gate, making it much more accessible to the public. The stately ancient structure, surrounded by imposing modern skyscrapers, was one of the most iconic images of the city. The gate was lit up at night, making for wonderful photos. Regular changing of the guard ceremonies took place there as well.

On Feb 10, 2008, a devastating fire severely damaged the gate's wooden superstructure. Restoration work is now underway.

✳ Seoul Fortress Walls

In the old days, Seoul was a typical medieval walled city, surrounded by an imposing stone wall controlled by a system of massive gates such as Sungnyemun. The walls were an impressive site, snaking along the ridge lines of surrounding mountains such as Mt. Namsan and Mt. Bukgaksan.

Although segments still exist, mostly high in the surrounding mountains, little is left of the old walls. In the area around Sungnyemun, the walls were dealt a decisive blow with the start of tram service in 1899. To make way for the tram tracks, the walls were pulled down, not just in Sungnyemun, but around Seoul's other main gates as well. The opening of tram service may have proven a major boon to Seoul's urban development, but it came at the price of an integral part of Seoul's history.

Recently, the Cultural Heritage Administration announced plans to rebuild sections of the old city walls as part of its push to turn the old downtown area into a UNESCO recognized historic site.

2✳ Taepyeongno and Samsung Complex

If Sungnyemun represents the Seoul of old, the grand skyscrapers of the **Samsung Complex** represent the Seoul of today.

Located just across and to the left of Sungnyemun Gate (facing City Hall), the Samsung Complex is the cor-

porate headquarters of
the Samsung Group, one
of Korea's most powerful
business conglomerates,
known as *jaebeol* in
Korean. The Samsung
Life Insurance Building,

built in the 1980s, is particularly noteworthy, covered as it
is in imported red granite, rare for buildings of its time.

Also part of the complex, located in the shadows of
Samsung's towering skyscrapers, is the uniquely designed
Rodin Gallery. Constructed mostly of glass, the gallery is
the permanent home to two of Rodin's sculptures and hosts
regular exhibits of Korean and international modern art. It
is closed on Mondays. The gallery is run by the Samsung
Foundation.

Interestingly enough, there's a small signpost in front of
the Rodin Gallery. The signpost marks the former location
of the **Jeonhwanguk**, Korea's first modern mint. As modernization pressures in the late 19th century grew, Korea's
traditional currency system—which was heavy and inconve-
nient to carry about—went into disorder, so in 1883, the
Jeonhwanguk was founded. The mint moved around quite
a bit as the crown and foreign powers fought over control
of the Korean economy. In 1892, the Japanese made a bid
to control Korean monetary policy by moving the mint to
foreigner-dominated Incheon, although it was later moved
back to Seoul—more specifically, Yongsan—in 1900.

Korea began printing paper money in 1903, but in
1904—thanks to the mass circulation of counterfeit money
and Japanese imperial policy—Korea's national finances
collapsed, the Jeonhwanguk was abolished, and Japan took
over Korea's money-making authority.

At any rate, it's said the Samsung Group chose the location for its corporate headquarters since it was, after all,
where money was made.

3❋ Bank of Korea Museum

Rather than head down Taepyeongno towards City Hall, swing a right and walk past the massive Namdaemun Market until you come to the entrance of Myeong-dong (marked by a strangely socialist-realist water fountain). At this intersection is one of Seoul's best collections of architecture from the Japanese occupation period.

The most obvious is the Renaissance-style **Bank of Korea Museum** (Historic Site No. 280). Started in 1908 and completed in 1912, the complex served first as the headquarters of the Bank of Choson, the central bank of Japan's Korean colony. The building was designed by pioneering Japanese architect Tatsuno Kingo, who also designed Tokyo Station and the Bank of Japan, which the Bank of Korea resembles. When Korea was liberated in 1945, the building became the headquarters of the newly established Bank of Korea. It is now a museum dedicated to the history of Korean banking and Korean currency. It's not a bad place to stroll around, actually, and the interior of the main hall is pretty spectacular (although no pictures are allowed inside).

The Bank of Korea Museum is a good example of the architectural style of Meiji Japan, when Japanese architects were sent to the West to study modern (read: Western) architectural styles and returned to build grand Renaissance and Baroque-style buildings in Japan and their colonies like Korea and Taiwan.

✦ Tatsuno Kingo

Tatsuno Kingo (1854–1919) was Japan's first modern architect. Born into a family of low-ranking samurai, Tatsuno studied modern architecture at Tokyo's Imperial College of Engineering (today's Department of Engineering at Tokyo University) under British expatriate architect Josiah Conder, who came to Japan in 1877. Graduating at the top of his class, he continued his studies in London, studying under the Gothic revival architect William Burges. Tatsuno played a major role in introducing Western-style architecture to Japan. His major works include the head-quarters of the Bank of Japan (1896), Manseibashi Station (1912), and Tokyo Station (1914). In Korea, the former Bank of Korea headquarters is his most notable work, although his influence can be felt in Seoul Station, which was designed by his student, Tsukamoto Yasushi.

4✦ Korea First Bank

On the other side of the fountain are Korea First Bank and the Shinsegae Department Store. Originally the Choson Savings Bank, the imposing neoclassical **Korea First Bank** was completed in 1933. Interestingly, it was the first building in Korea whose design was selected by open competition. Three conditions were attached to  proposals—the building should have a safe, it should have a hall the masses could use freely, and it should have a roof-top restaurant for bank employees. In two months, some 269 proposals were received from within and without

Korea, many coming from Japan. Eventually, a proposal by Tokyo architect Hirabayashi Kingyo was selected.

In 1945, the building was taken over by Korea First Bank, which used it as its headquarters until 1987, when the bank built a new headquarters in Jongno. Korea First Bank (now Standard Chartered First Bank Korea) still uses the building, however. In addition to its spectacular neo-classical exterior, with its four Doric columns, the interior of the main lobby has been well preserved.

5⚬ Shinsegae Department Store

Next to Korea First Bank is **Shinsegae Department Store**. The Shinsegae Department Store is Seoul's last remaining Japanese occupation-era department store. It was founded in 1930 as the Seoul branch of the Mitsukoshi Department Store, one of Japan's best known department store chains. After 1945, the building saw a number of different uses until it was purchased by the Samsung Group, who turned it into the Shinsegae Department Store.

The department store is a luxurious Renaissance-style building that was recently remodeled, although its original exterior has been kept intact. For some good views of the surrounding neighborhood, check out the roof-top garden.

6⚬ Hwangudan and the Chosun Hotel

From the Bank of Korea Museum, head left until you come to the Westin Chosun Hotel. Tucked away in the hotel's rear garden is one of Seoul's truly hidden gems, the **Hwangudan** (**Wongudan**), or Altar of Heaven (Historic Site No. 157).

The three-story octagonal shrine Hwangungu outwardly resembles the great Temple of Heaven in Beijing. It also served the same function. Following China's defeat by Japan in the first Sino-Japanese War, Korea's vassal rela-

tionship with China was severed, and in 1897, King Gojong elevated his status to that of emperor, placing him on equal footing with the Chinese emperor. Accordingly, it fell upon the new emperor to perform the Rite of Heaven, a sacred ritual in which the emperor would pray on the behalf of his people for a bountiful harvest. The ritual had been discontinued in Korea in 1464, after which Korea's kings deferred to the Son of Heaven, i.e., the Chinese emperor, to perform the rite.

To perform the Rite of Heaven, a large altar complex was constructed in 1899. Unfortunately, most of the complex was destroyed in 1913 by the Japanese, who built in its place the Chosun Railway Hotel. All that remains of the former altar is the Hwangungu, the three-story octagonal shrine where memorial tablets were enshrined. Three stone drums remain as well.

Like Sungnyemun Gate, the Hwangudan cuts a dramatic figure against a backdrop of skyscrapers and electronic signboards. The Westin Chosun Hotel, meanwhile, is a historic site in its own right, built to replace the Chosun Railway Hotel, Korea's first international-class luxury hotel.

7❋ Seoul City Hall

The nerve center of one of the world's most dynamic cities, **Seoul City Hall** (Registered Cultural Property No. 52) is also one of Seoul's most significant pieces of architecture from the Japanese occupation era.

Seoul's city hall was originally built on Mt. Namsan in 1885, but was later moved to the former Japanese consulate in 1895. Urban development and an increasing population dictated a newer, larger complex be built, so in 1925, work began on a new city hall. Construction was completed in 1926. The result was an imposing, almost menacing gray building. Employing a Spartan architectural style loved by many a 20th century dictator, its mass, lack of exterior decoration and row upon row of windows intimidate the viewer. Even with the skyscrapers of nearby Mugyo-dong looming over it, the building still retains its power. Albert Speer would have been impressed.

Architecturally, the complex is an example of "eclecticism," a creative mixing and matching of Eastern and Western architectural styles frequently employed by Japanese architects of the time. The building, in fact, incorporates a number of motifs from the Japanese Diet Building in Tokyo, including the tower roof and window arrangement. To the viewer, the exterior appears to be made of stone, but it is, in fact, mortared brick.

A number of controversial theories have been associated with Seoul City Hall. The most frequently repeated one is that it and the old Capitol Building (demolished in 1996) were designed in the shape of the Chinese characters for Japan. Experts do not believe this to be true, at least in the case of Seoul City Hall, but the story persists.

A new, state-of-the-art City Hall building is now being built—the new design will incorporate the façade and lobby of the historic old building, which will be renovated as a public library. Construction of the new City Hall is scheduled for completion in 2011.

8 Seoul Plaza

Not long ago, the area in front of Seoul City Hall was one of Korea's busiest traffic rotaries. In 2004, however, the traffic rotary was replaced by an oval grass field as part of then-  Seoul Mayor Lee Myung-bak's program to beautify the city. It is now a popular lunchtime and weekend retreat.

9 Seoul Municipal Council Building

Almost directly across Taepyeongno from Seoul City Hall is the **Seoul Municipal Council Building** (Registered Cultural Property No. 11), easily recognizable as a white, three-story building with a distinctive tower. Originally built in 1933 and modeled on Hibiya Public Hall in Tokyo (one of Japan's oldest performing arts venues), Seoul Municipal Council Building was originally built as a cultural hall. After Liberation, it was used to hold Korea's constitutional assembly, and became Korea's first National Assembly Building, where the country's first president was

 elected. It was also the scene of some of Korea's lower moments, for example, when a very annoyed gangster-turned-lawmaker chose to protest parliamentary corruption by splashing buckets of pig urine on the chamber walls.

10 ❈ Cheonggyecheon Plaza

Heading up towards Gwanghwamun from Seoul City Hall, you'll come to **Cheonggyecheon Plaza**, which marks the head of the restored Cheonggyecheon Stream. The waterway, originally formed from tributary streams that flowed down from Seoul's surrounding mountains, was covered over by concrete in the 1960s. In September 2005, however, the stream was re-opened to the public following an ambitious restoration project.

You'll know you've reached Cheonggyecheon Plaza when you see "Spring," a 20 meter high blue and red sculpture in the shape of a marsh snail by American pop artists Claes Oldenburg and Coosje van Bruggen.

11 ❈ Old Dong-A Ilbo Building (Ilmin Museum of Art)

The **Ilmin Museum of Art**, located right next door to the Cheonggyecheon Stream, served as the headquarters of the Dong-A Ilbo newspaper from 1926 to 1992. Built in Renaissance style, the structure has undergone several extensions and renovations. Note the ornate decorations around the door and windows and the beautiful bay window. Overlooking the Ilmin Museum of Art is the **Dong-A Media Center,** a steel and glass skyscraper completed in 2000. The contrast between the old and new is one of Seoul's most defining characteristics.

❋ Skyscrapers of Downtown Seoul

From Seoul City Hall to Gwanghwamun, you'll find an assortment of skyscrapers and other high-rise buildings. With Korea's rapid economic development kicking off in the 1960s, the area around Taepyeongno and Gwanghwamun found itself home to many tall buildings to house government offices, newspapers, financial companies, and other commercial enterprises. The skyscraper construction boom has continued straight up to the present day, so the neighborhood is a good place to sample typical building styles from the 1970s, 1980s, 1990s and 21st century.

12❋ Sejong-no, Korea's Nerve Center

The area along **Sejong-no Boulevard,** stretching from the Gwanghwamun Intersection to Gwanghwamun Gate, was referred to as the "six ministry street" (*yukjo geori*) during the Joseon era, for it was here that the royal ministries were located. Little has changed since then; along Sejong-no you'll now find the Ministry of Foreign Affairs and Trade, Central Government Complex, Ministry of Culture and

Bigak   Sejong Center for the Performing Arts

Tourism, Ministry of Information and Communications and other important government ministries and agencies. You'll also find several important cultural venues, including the imposing Sejong Center for the Performing Arts and the Kyobo Book Store.

There are representative examples of Korean architecture from several different decades here, ranging from the 1970s (the US Embassy and Ministry of Culture and Tourism) to the 21st century (Ministry of Foreign Affairs and Trade). Due to the lack of knowhow and resources that plagued Korea during its development process, many of the buildings in this neighborhood were designed by foreign architectural firms, although the newer buildings were designed by Koreans.

The Sejong Center for the Performing Arts was completed in 1978 to replace the old Seoul Cultural Hall, which burnt down in a fire in 1972. Designed by architect Eom Deok-mun, the building uses modern architectural techniques and materials to express Korean traditional architectural concepts and motifs.

❋ Gwanghwamun Plaza

The are around Sejongno Boulevard is currently undergoing a major facelift to transform it into a pedestrian-friendly culture and leisure space. The new space, which will include water fountains, ponds, and a grand statue of King Sejong the Great, is set to open from August 2009.

13❋ Gwanghwamun Gate: Main Gate to the Main Palace

At the far north end of Sejong-no is **Gwanghwamun Gate**. The gate, currently undergoing renovation, served as the main entrance to the Gyeongbokgung Palace. The gate was originally built in 1395, although the name "Gwanghwamun" dates from 1426. The name means "The grand virtue of the king shines upon the entire nation."

Gwanghwamun Gate has experienced several ups and

downs in the recent past. In 1927, the Japanese moved the gate from the south wall to the east wall of the palace to make way for the massive Government-General Building. Destroyed in the Korean War, it was rebuilt in 1968, but this time using concrete instead of stone. Besides the concrete, there were other issues with the 1968 restoration as well. The new gate was 14.5 meters north of the original location, and its angle was slightly off. The original gate was built parallel to the throne room of the Gyeongbokgung Palace, but the 1963 restoration was built parallel to the former Government-General Building, which lay in between the gate and the throne room. This led to the gate being 5.6 degrees off the central axis of the palace.

The current restoration work on the gate, which should be completed by 2009, will restore the gate to its original position, allowing the gate to finally rest at ease, free of its painful past.

14❋ Gyeongbokgung Palace

The **Gyeongbokgung Palace** (Historic Site No. 117) was first built in 1395, although the current palace dates from an

1865 reconstruction. The palace is a mere shadow of what it was prior to Japan's occupation of Korea, when the Japanese dismantled many of its buildings.

The Gyeongbokgung was Seoul's largest royal palace and is a truly remarkable place to stroll around. Restoration work is always ongoing to restore the palace to a semblance of its original state. See Chapter 5 ("19th Century Royal Residences II") for a fuller description of the palace complex.

❋ National Palace Museum of Korea

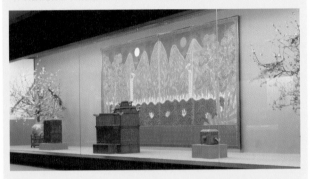

The **National Palace Museum of Korea,** located on the grounds of Gyeongbokgung Palace, used to house the National Museum of Korea from the time the old museum (formerly the Japanese occupation-era Government-General building) was demolished in 1995–1996 and the present museum (located in Yongsan) was opened in 2007. It is now dedicated to housing artifacts from the old royal court of Joseon.

The roots of the National Palace Museum of Korea go back to 1992, when the Royal Museum was opened in Deoksugung Palace. The Royal Museum soon outgrew its old home, but fortunately, the move of the National Museum freed up the perfect venue. The current museum opened on Nov 27, 2007.

The National Palace Museum houses some 40,000 artifacts, including priceless works of art and fascinating relics that provide insight into the lives of Korea's kings.

15 ✦ Dongsipjagak Watchtower

The **Dongsipjagak** (Seoul Tangible Cultural Property No. 13) is another spectacular example of Korean traditional architecture meeting Japanese colonial urban planning. The Dongsipjagak, which dates to 1865, was one of two watchtowers that guarded the wall of the Gyeongbokgung Palace. Unfortunately, when the Japanese made way for the Government-General Building, a massive European-style building built to house the colonial government, they moved the Gwanghwamun Gate to the northeast and tore down the palace wall, turning the Dongsipjagak into a traffic island. And so it remains today.

Linguistically, however, the Dongsipjagak does remind us of the true meaning of the Korean word for palace complex, *gunggwol*. *Gung* means palace, while *gwol* refers to the raised watchtowers that guarded the palace entrance.

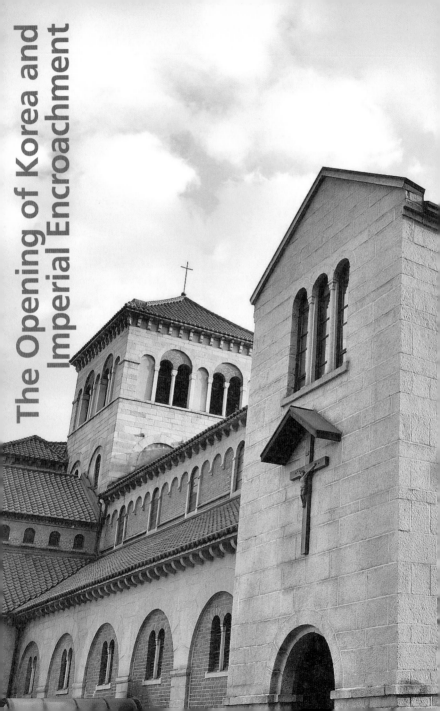
The Opening of Korea and Imperial Encroachment

TOUR* 2

The Opening of Korea and Imperial Encroachment

Jeong-dong Area

Located just behind Deoksugung Palace, the Jeong-dong neighborhood was at one time the center of Korea's foreign community, a district of foreign legations and Christian churches. Even today, the area has a distinctively exotic feel, its quiet tree-lined alleyways home to a collection of handsome Western-style buildings, a legacy of Korea's first Western missionaries, diplomats and educators. Still, it's hard not to walk through Jeong-dong without a heavy heart. It was in this neighborhood that the Joseon era's dramatic endgame was played out, a game which concluded with the death of Korean independence and decades of brutal Japanese colonial rule. The Westerners may have brought modern education and medicine, but—as symbolized by the tower of the old Russian legation—they also brought imperial ambitions. More than any other area of Seoul, Jeong-dong speaks of a time when Korea was the object of intense competition amongst the great imperial powers of the West and Japan, when Korea's fate was decided not in the royal court, but in the smoky backrooms of foreign legations.

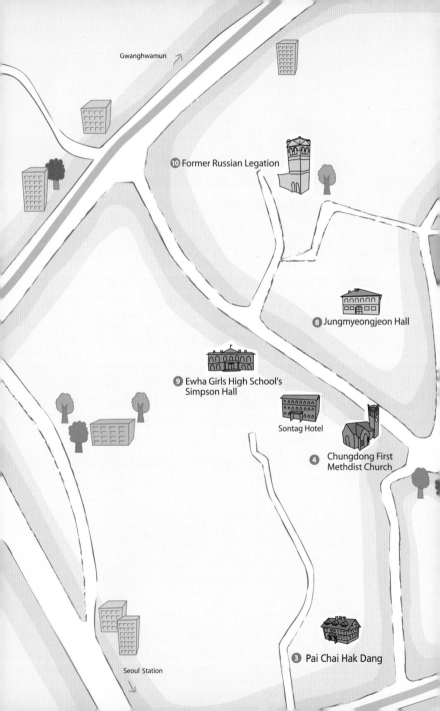

Gwanghwamun

10 Former Russian Legation

8 Jungmyeongjeon Hall

9 Ewha Girls High School's Simpson Hall

Sontag Hotel

4 Chungdong First Methdist Church

Seoul Station

3 Pai Chai Hak Dang

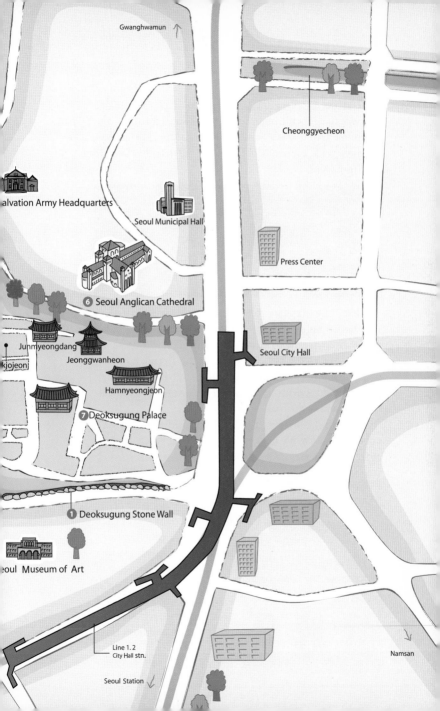

Gwanghwamun ↑

Cheonggyecheon

Salvation Army Headquarters

Seoul Municipal Hall

Press Center

6 Seoul Anglican Cathedral

Junmyeongdang

Jeonggwanheon

kjojeon

Seoul City Hall

Hamnyeongjeon

7 Deoksugung Palace

1 Deoksugung Stone Wall

eoul Museum of Art

Line 1. 2
City Hall stn.

Namsan ↓

Seoul Station ↓

1❋ Deoksugung Stone Wall

Next to the Deoksugung's Daehanmun Gate is a quaint alleyway lined by the outer wall of Deoksugung Palace. The handsome **Deoksugung Stone Wall**, or *doldam*, makes for a romantic walk, especially in fall, when the trees that line the alley turn color.

While a popular date course, the Deoksugung Stone Wall does have a rather ominous urban legend attached to it. It's said that couples who stroll along the alley will break up once they reach the end. The origin of this legend, however, is quite simple—not so long ago, Seoul Family Court, where Seoul residents would go to get divorced, was located at the end of the road.

If you look down at the brick-lined alleyway, you'll notice plaques with images of Jeong-dong's rich modern architectural legacy.

2❋ Seoul Museum of Art
(Former Supreme Court Building)

Built by the Japanese in 1928 as the Keijo (the Japanese name for Seoul) Court House, the **Seoul Museum of Art** (Registered Cultural Property No. 237) would become the model for many other public buildings built during the colonial era—see, for example, the former main building of Seoul National University in Daehangno, now used as the office of Arts Council Korea.

After Liberation in 1945, the building became the Supreme Court of Korea. In 1995, however, the Supreme Court moved to Seocho-dong south of the river, and the structure was extensively remodeled for use as the Seoul Museum of Art. Given the historical importance of the building, however, it was decided to keep the beautiful façade of the old court.

The old court building makes for a pleasant resting spot, set atop a small hillock and surrounded by beautiful gardens.

3※ Pai Chai Hak Dang

Not far from the Seoul Museum of Art is the former **East Hall of Pai Chai Hak Dang**, Korea's first modern intermediate school (and the predecessor of Pai Chai Middle and High School). The school was founded in 1886 by American Methodist missionary Henry Gerhard Appenzeller, who also founded Chungdong First Methodist Church just down the street.

The American imprint in Jeong-dong is quite strong as American missionaries were responsible for establishing many of Korea's first modern schools and medical facilities. The United States was, in fact, the first Western nation to establish a diplomatic presence in Korea, opening its legation in Seoul in 1883. In Jeong-dong alone, the American legacy can be seen in Pai Chai Hak Dang, First Methodist Church, Ewha Hak Dang and Habib House (the site of the old US legation, now the US ambassador's residence, which you cannot enter).

The East Hall of Pai Chai Hak Dang, with its red brick symmetrical construction, has been well preserved and is a wonderful example of early 20th century missionary school architecture. The current building was built in 1916. A major restoration was completed in 2007.

4❋ Chungdong First Methodist Church

A little further down the road from Pai Chai Hak Dang is a simple Victorian Gothic church made of red brick. This church is **Chungdong First Methodist Church** (Historical Site No. 256), and is a major symbol of the early American influence in Korea.

Chungdong First Methodist Church, Korea's first Methodist church, was built in 1898, but later enlarged in 1926. The original design of the church has changed little, making it an outstanding example of early Protestant church architecture in Korea. Indeed, the church is the oldest Western-style house of worship in Korea.

The church was founded by the afore-mentioned American missionary Henry Gerhard Appenzeller, who came to Korea in 1885 at the age of 27. Appenzeller, a Pennsylvania native, was a major figure in the history of Korean Christianity—along with Presbyterian missionary

(and fellow American) Horace Underwood, he brought Protestant Christianity to Korea. Also like Underwood and Presbyterian missionary (and first US consul to Korea) Horace Allen, Appenzeller's missionary activities included social work, including the opening of Korea's first modern schools. Unfortunately for Appenzeller, his activity would catch up with him—in 1902, at the age of 44, he drowned during a trip to far-off Mokpo to attend a Bible translation conference.

Appenzeller first set up shop in a Korean-style *hanok* (which he called Bethel Chapel), but when his flock surpassed 200, he decided a new church was needed. That new church is the current Chungdong First Methodist Church. Similar in style to many American brick churches, Chungdong First Methodist Church was designed by a Japanese architect, although a Korean architect may have assisted in the design. The church also transformed to reflect social change. Originally, the prayer hall was divided in two by a curtain, with women on one side and men on the other. By the late 1910s, however, the curtain was removed, marking a major change in the role of women in Korean society.

5※ Salvation Army Headquarters

One of the hidden gems of the Jeong-dong neighborhood is the **Salvation Army Headquarters**.

Just follow the Deoksugung Stone Wall past the US Ambassador's Residence (the alley has a high security pres-

ence, so you can't miss it) and you'll eventually come to a massive neo-classical brick building. This is the Salvation Army Headquarters, built in 1926 to mark the 70th birthday of

Bramwell Booth, the second General of the Salvation Army and son of Salvation Army founder William Booth.

When it was built, the imposing red-brick structure was one of Seoul's 10 largest buildings. A two-story building, the entrance is marked by four large columns.

The Salvation Army is a Christian charity and church founded by former Methodist minister William Booth and his wife Catherine in 1865. True to its name, the Salvation Army adopted a military-style organization, being led by "generals" and "officers." The Salvation Army Headquarters in Seoul served as the center of the group's charity and social projects in Korea and trained local officers.

Unfortunately, the beautiful building doesn't see many visitors due to its relatively hidden location.

6❀ Seoul Anglican Cathedral

Korea has many old churches, but few can match **Seoul Anglican Cathedral** in terms of its beauty.

Located near the British Embassy, the Seoul Anglican Cathedral is the central church of the Seoul Diocese and the central church of the Anglican Church of Korea. It's an awe-inspiringly beautiful building, easily recognized by its Romanesque structure and orange Korean roof tiles.

The third Anglican bishop of Korea, Mark Trollope, consecrated the present church in 1926. The history of the Anglican church in Jeong-dong, however, goes back much earlier, to when Korea's first Anglican Bishop, John Corfe, came to Korea in 1890 and established a *hanok* church in an old royal educational institute.

Seoul Anglican Cathedral was the first cathedral to be built in Romanesque style in the Far East. The church, built in the shape of a Latin cross, was designed by British architect Arthur Dixon. Like many Anglican churches, the cathedral incorporates Korean architectural elements, including elevated eaves, granite walls, window frames and roofing with Korean tiles. In this regard, the church doesn't appear all too out-of-place next to Deoksugung Palace.

The interior is just as splendid as the exterior—be sure to check out the beautiful gold mosaics by the altar (painted in 1931 by British Arts and Crafts designer George Jack). Also note the wooden trusses on the ceiling. In the basement is a small crypt where Bishop Mark Trollope is buried (English-language services are held in the crypt as well).

When the church was first consecrated, it was in truth only half-completed. So it remained until 1993, when Dixon's original plans were discovered by chance in a library in Lexington. The expansion work was completed in 1996.

Also on the grounds are some beautiful priest quarters that mix Korean and Western styles (brick buildings with Korean roofs).

7 ✸ Deoksugung Palace

Deoksugung Palace (Historical Site No. 124), the centerpiece of the Jeong-dong neighborhood, was the stage upon which the fall of the Daehan Empire was played out. As beautiful as it is, it's hard to stroll among its gardens without a sense of tragedy.

Deoksugung Palace was originally the home of King Seonjo's older brother, Prince Wolsan, until it was made a temporary palace following the Japanese invasion of 1592, when the other palaces in the capital were burned to the ground. In 1623, King Injo moved the royal residence to the Changdeokgung, so for the next 270 years, Deoksugung was used as an auxiliary palace.

The fate of Deoksugung would change, however, in 1897, when King Gojong—returning from a year's sojourn at the Russian Legation—moved into Deoksugung Palace, under the watchful eye of the Western (and especially Russian) legations.

For the next decade, the palace would be the scene of much drama as Gojong struggled to modernize his kingdom while staving off the imperial advances of Japan and the West. Even after Gojong abdicated the throne under Japanese pressure in 1907, he continued to reside in the palace, dying there in 1919.

Unlike Seoul's other palaces, Deoksugung has a large number of Western-style structures, including the impressive Seokjojeon Hall. There are also several older, Korean-style buildings that are not well known but are of immense architectural value.

❈ Hamnyeongjeon Hall

The **Hamnyeongjeon Hall** (Treasure No. 820) was the bed chamber of King Gojong. The original structure was burnt down in 1904 when a great fire swept through the palace; the current structure dates from a reconstruction undertaken that year. It was also in this hall that King Gojong passed away on Jan 22, 1919. His death proved a spark to the March 1 Independence Movement that would break out that year.

In most ways, the Hamnyeongjeon Hall is a typical royal sleeping chamber, although the gargoyles on the roof — called *japsang*—are quite unusual for such a building. The gargoyles are put on the building to frighten evil spirits away.

❈ Seogeodang Hall

The **Seogeodang Hall** is easily recognizable—it's the only two-story building on the palace grounds. It's also a *baek-gol* (White Skeleton) structure, meaning it's unpainted.

The Seogeodang Hall, too was burnt down during the fire of 1904, and rebuilt that year.

❋ Jeukjodang Hall and Junmyeongdang Hall

 Behind the Seogeodang Hall are the **Jeukjodang Hall** and **Junmyeongdang Hall**. The two halls are connected by a corridor, with the Jeukjodang Hall on the right and the Junmyeongdang Hall on the left.

King Gojong lived in the Junmyeongdang Hall for some time. He also used it to receive foreign dignitaries. Jeukjodang Hall was the place for crowning the king.

❋ Seokjojeon Hall, East Hall

The Deoksugung Palace complex is actually two palaces in one—a Korean palace and a Western-style palace. The Western-style palace is immediately recognizable from its imposing neo-classical buildings and Western-style fountain surrounded by a Western-style garden.

The **Seokjojeon Hall**—or at least its East Wing—was built between 1900 and 1910. Construction of the building was originally pushed by a Briton, Sir John McLeavy Brown, who was at the time serving as financial adviser to the Korean Imperial Government. It was originally supposed to be built at Gyeonghuigung Palace, but Brown insisted on its present location within Deoksugung, quite possibly because it was right next to the British Legation (back then, the palace had a western gate directly facing the front gate of the legation).

Brown entrusted the design of the building to a compatriot, G.R. Harding, while the interior was designed by another Briton by the name of Lovell. Material and equipment for the job were imported from Great Britain.

In 1905, however, Japan won the Russo-Japanese War, so out went the Western advisers and in came the Japanese. As chief financial adviser to the Emperor, Brown was replaced by Baron Megata Tanetaro, the Harvard-educated father of Japan's modern tax system. Megata was awarded construction rights for the Seokjojeon upon receiving his appointment.

Likewise, the supervising architect position changed hands frequently—it started with Korean architect Sim Ui-seok, and then passed to Russian architect Aleksey Seredin-Sabatin, a Japanese by the name of Ogawa, and finally a Briton, M. H. Davidson.

Although it was built as a home for the Korean imperial household, it never actually served as one, although Gojong did reside there during his retirement.

The Japanese eventually turned the Seokjojeon into an art gallery. After Liberation, it was the venue for the Joint American-Soviet Commission in 1945. After the Korean War, it became the National Museum of Korea, a role it served until 1986. It's now part of the Royal Museum, which displays artifacts from the Joseon royal family.

Take note of the façade—the plum flower became the symbol of the royal family following the modernization reforms of 1894.

❀ Seokjojeon Hall, West Hall

The **West Wing**, designed by Japanese "colonial" architect Nakamura Yoshihei, was built
in two short years between 1937 and 1939.

Why the rush, you might ask?

Well, in 1933, the Deoksugung was
opened to the public, and the Royal
Household Museum (Korea's first museum,
originally located at the Changgyeonggung)
was to be moved to the Seokjojeon. As it
would turn out, however, the Seokjojeon
instead became an art museum, which
annoyed the Korean royal family, who at
this point had been integrated (at least officially) into the Japanese peerage system.

As an act of appeasement, the colonial
authorities hurriedly constructed a massive western wing,
which became the so-called Yi Royal Family Museum.

The building is now used as the National Museum of
Art, Deoksugung.

❀ Jeonggwanheon Pavilion

Designed by Aleksey
Seredin-Sabatin, a Russian
architect in the employ of
the Korean government, the
Jeonggwanheon Pavilion
was built as a rest and
relaxation place for King
Gojong, who enjoyed
lounging on the pavilion with a good cup of coffee, then a
rare foreign import.

The pavilion—which is believed to have been built
around 1900—is a queer architectural creation, mixing
Korean and Romanesque elements. Particularly noteworthy
are the colorful and intricate designs on the pavilion's
wooden railings.

8❋ Jungmyeongjeon Hall

The **Jungmyeongjeon Hall**, built in 1900, was a royal library and banquet hall for foreign envoys designed by the aforementioned Seredin-Sabatin. It has the honor of being the first Western-style building built on the grounds of a Korean palace. Historically, it's quite important as the site where the Protectorate Treaty of 1905 was concluded, under which Korea signed away its foreign policy decision-making to Japan. Originally part of the Deoksugung, the stone wall separating it from the palace was built during the colonial era. Recently, however, the Cultural Heritage Administration placed the building back within the grounds of the Deoksugung...at least administratively.

9❋ Ewha Girls High School's Simpson Hall

Ewha Girls High School's **Simpson Hall** (built in 1915) is all that is left of the original Ewha Hak Dang, which was founded in 1886 by American Methodist Episcopal missionary Mary F. Scranton. Ewha Hak Dang would eventually grow into Ewha Middle and High School and, of course, Ewha Womens University, the world's largest women's university.

With its red brick and keystones, the school would serve as a model for many other Christian schools built during the first half of the 20th century.

Interestingly, on the grounds of Ewha Girls High School

is the site of the **former Sontag Hotel** (designed by Seredin-Sabatin), which was Seoul's first Western-style hotel and a major meeting spot (and scheming venue) of late Joseon-era Seoul's foreign community. The hotel was founded by Antoinette Sontag, the daughter-in-law of Russian Consul to Korea, Karl Ivanovich Weber. It was Sontag who introduced coffee to Korea—King Gojong picked up a taste for it while he was residing in the Russian consulate.

10 ❊ Former Russian Legation

On a hill strategically overlooking Jeong-dong and the Deoksugung Palace is the site of the **former Russian Legation**. Unfortunately, most of the original compound was destroyed during the Korean War. All that remains is the Renaissance-style central tower. The original compound was built in 1890, and like some of the other buildings mentioned here, it was designed by Russian architect Seredin-Sabatin.

The compound is of intense historical interest, and is symbolic of the crisis faced by the Korean kingdom in the years leading up to the nation's colonization by Japan. On Oct 8, 1895, Empress Myeongseong was murdered by Japanese ruffians at the Gyeongbokgung Palace. King

Gojong, feeling the Japanese threat, decided in February the following year to flee the palace together with the crown prince, taking refuge in the Russian Legation, where Gojong was friends with the Russian minister, Karl Ivanovich Weber. Gojong stayed in the Russian Legation for an entire year, during which time Moscow exerted tremendous influence on the Korean government. It was a humiliating time for the nation, and proved the folly of over-relying on one power to ward off the aggression of another.

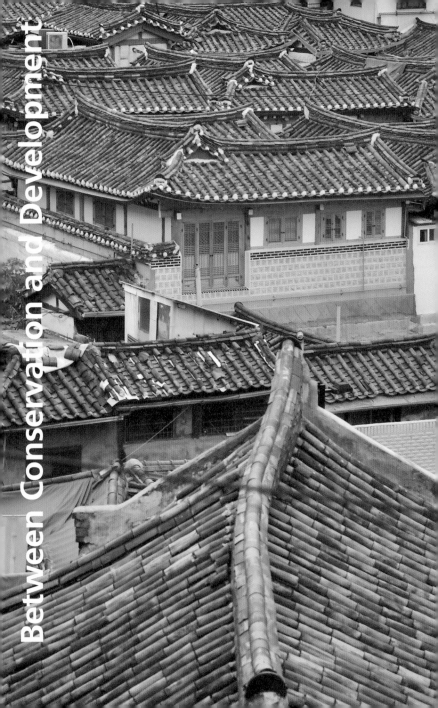

Between Conservation and Development

TOUR 3

Between Conservation and Development

Bukchon

Bukchon, or "North Village," is the neighborhood of Seoul on the lower slopes of Mt. Bugaksan between Gyeongbokgung and Changdeokgung palaces. Owing to its location between the palaces and its outstanding natural scenery—the neighborhood overlooks downtown Seoul with Mt. Namsan forming something of a natural "folding screen"—it used to be the exclusive residential preserve of members of the Joseon royal family and high palace officials. Due to social and economic conditions in the latter part of the colonial period, however, more and more families began building homes in Bukchon, leading to the high concentration of *hanok* homes that we see today.

Thanks to its plethora of *hanok* homes and cozy alleyways, the area is a major tourist drawing card that Seoul Metropolitan Government has been keen to exploit. At the same time, tourist and commercial development and a government restoration project have brought their own problems. Today, Bukchon is a prime example of the conflict between preservation and development.

While this walk will focus mostly on Bukchon, we will also visit Seoul Fortress, the remnants of which can still be found high in the mountains of northern Seoul, Byeonsachang armory and Choong Ang High School, a beautiful example of Gothic revival architecture and important piece of Korea's early modern cultural heritage.

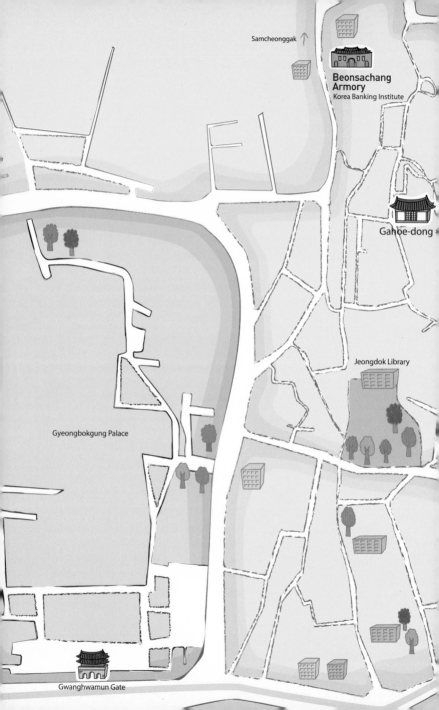

Samcheonggak ↑

Beonsachang Armory
Korea Banking Institute

Gahoe-dong →

Jeongdok Library

Gyeongbokgung Palace

Gwanghwamun Gate

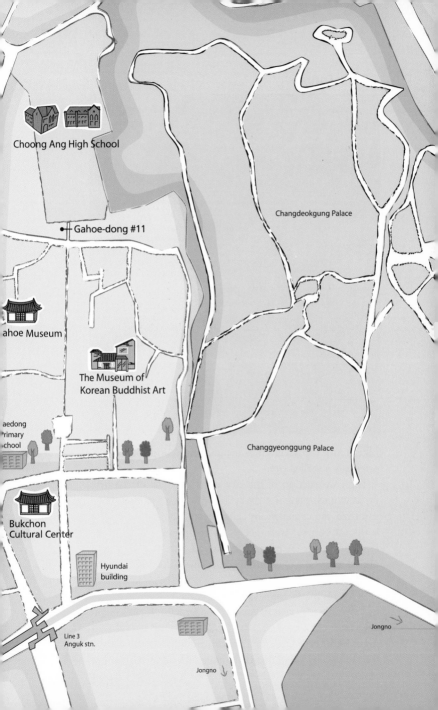

❋ Seoul Fortress

Like many medieval cities around the world, Seoul was originally a walled city.

The construction of the city walls was one of the first projects undertaken by the fledgling Joseon kingdom once it moved the capital from Gaesong to Seoul in 1394. The walls, of course, were necessary for protecting the new kingdom from enemies both foreign and domestic, and played a key role in controlling movement in and out of the royal capital.

Work on the fortress wall began in the first lunar month of 1396, the fifth year of Joseon founder King Taejo's reign. After a royal survey, it was decided the wall would ring some 59,500 *cheok* (around 19km) around the new capital, linking the city's four guardian mountains—Mt. Baegaksan,

Mt. Inwangsan, Mt. Mokmyeoksan (now called Mt. Namsan) and Mt. Naksan.

It was a monumental project—some 118,000 laborers were drafted from all over the country. The wall itself was divided into 97 sections, each section named after a character in the Qian Zi Wen ("1,000 Character Essay," used as a basic reading textbook in Confucian China and Korea). An official was put in charge of each section—they would etch their names into the stones of the wall, traces of which can still be seen today.

On the rough, high mountain sections, the stone walls were 15 *cheok* (4.8m) high. These stone sections accounted for some 19,200 *cheok* (6.1km) of the wall. In flat low-lying areas, the wall was made of clay. These walls were 25 *cheok* wide (about 7.6m) at the base and 18 *cheok* (5.7m) at the top and accounted for 40,300 *cheok* (6.1km) of the total walls. Along the Cheonggyecheon Stream, a water gate was built.

This wasn't enough for the new king, however, so in winter of that year, he drafted another 80,000 laborers to replace some of the clay sections of the wall with stone. It was at this time that Seoul's four massive gates—Heunginmun to the east (now Dongdaemun), Donuimun to the west, Sungnyemun (now Namdaemun) to the south, and Sukcheongmun to the north—were completed. Four smaller gates, including Gwanghuimun and Changuimun, were completed at this time as well.

The city walls underwent another major reconstruction in 1422, when all of the wall's clay sections were replaced with stone. The wall was heightened as well. This project required a labor force of 322,000 men. Further renovations were undertaken in 1704, and in 1743 and 1869.

In 1910, however, Korea was annexed by Japan, and the new colonial authorities viewed the city walls as an impediment to Seoul's development as a modern city. The walls were torn down to make way for tram tracks and road—all that remains now are the Heunginmun, Sungnyemun and

Sukcheongmun gates, some of the smaller gates and sections of fortress wall in the mountains. If you're willing to do a bit of hiking, you can see the 10.5km of remaining wall. Ironically, the preservation of these sections of the wall has been helped by the political tensions between North and South Korea. Until recently, much of the fortress walls in the mountains north of downtown Seoul were declared militarily sensitive areas after a failed North Korean commando raid on the presidential palace in 1968, and were placed off-limits to the general public. Even today, as you hike along the fortress wall, you can see many military facilities dotting the hillsides and soldiers patrolling iron fences that run alongside the old stone walls. In this regard, the fortress walls have never ceased in their original function—to protect the capital from attack.

In 2006, the Korean government announced plans to restore lost sections of the old city wall as part of a bid to register the downtown area with UNESCO. The restoration project would take some 10 years.

✳ Beonsachang Armory

An interesting little piece of Korea's early modern history can be found on the grounds of the Korea Banking Institute in Samcheong-dong. This building, the **Beonsachang**, was Korea's first modern armory, built by Chinese laborers in 1884.

This was just a few years after Japan had forced Korea to open up with a little gunboat diplomacy, employing modern weapons that Korea lacked.

Designed (presumably) by a Chinese architect, the building reveals both Chinese and Western architectural styles. Note, for example, the Western-style doors and windows and German-style wooden truss ceiling. In the late 19th century, Chinese-style brick buildings were seen as a sign of modernity.

Although the building was built as a modern arms factory, when 38 Korean students returned home from studying

modern weapon-making skills at a factory in Tianjin, China, they found they still lacked the capability to build guns. Korea ended up importing weapons and using the Beonsachang to repair them when they broke.

During the Japanese occupation period, the building was used as a germ research center, a role it continued under the post-war US military administration. It was then converted into a social welfare research center before being transferred to the Bank of Korea and attached to the Korea Banking Institute.

When this armory was restored in 1984, an inscription found on one of the roof beams said that it was built in 1884 during the reign of King Gojong (1863-1907) of the Joseon kingdom (1392-1910) for the manufacture of cast-iron parts for weapons production. It was constructed eight years after Korea opened its door to Japan with the signing of the Treaty of Ganghwa in 1876, when the government was striving to build up a modern military. The walls are made of dark grey bricks and have a stripe of red bricks around the top. The roof is gabled and the doors arched. The frame of the front door is of granite. The frames of the side doors are adorned with stripeds of red brick.

❋ Choong Ang High School

Choong Ang High School was founded in 1908 by a group promoting Korean education, ostensibly for non-political reasons but more than likely to promote national development and national independence, which was under threat at the time. After the founding group was disbanded by the Japanese in 1910, it was taken over by the Young Korean Academy (a.k.a. the "Heungsadahn"), the San Francisco-based civic group founded by Korean independence activist Dosan Ahn Chang-ho. The school ran into management difficulties, however, and in 1915, it was bought out by none other than Kim Song-su.

❋ Kim Song-su

Educator. Journalist. Statesman. Father of Korean capitalism. Early proponent of liberal democracy in Korea.

And, depending on your particular point of view, Japanese collaborator.

Born into a family of wealthy Jeollabuk-do landowners in 1891, Kim purchased Choong Ang High School in 1915, just after returning to Korea with a degree in political economy from

Kim Song-su

Japan's Waseda University. He founded the Dong-A Ilbo in 1920, and bought Korea University in 1932 (which, like Choong Ang High School, had been founded to promote Korean education, and like Choong Ang High School, had fallen into management difficulties). He spent the war years promoting the Japanese war effort (or so he is accused), but after Japan's surrender, he ended up an adviser to the US Military Government in Korea. He eventually founded the Korea Democratic Party (the ancestor of today's Democratic Party) and became Korea's second vice president in 1951 before resigning the next year over President Syngman Rhee's dictatorial tendencies (or because of a stroke). He died three years later in 1955.

The **Main Hall**, commissioned by Kim and designed by one of the fathers of Korean modern architecture, Park Dong-jin, was completed in 1937. Those who have been to Korea University will no doubt notice the similarities—the Korea University main hall and library were designed by the same architect at the commission of the same man. It's a pretty Gothic-style building, and wouldn't look completely out of place on a US university campus. Particularly beauti-

ful are the Tudor arch and the imposing castle-like tower. From the front door, you get a nice view of N Seoul Tower in the background.

The interior courtyard of the school is also a thing of beauty. To the left and right are the **West Hall** and **East Hall**, built in 1921 and 1923, respectively. The buildings were designed by Japanese colonial architect Nakamura Yoshihei, who also designed Cheondogyo Central Temple near Insa-dong.

✳ Bukchon

Between the Gyeongbokgung and Changdeokgung palaces, nestled on the slopes of Mt. Bugaksan, is one of Seoul's most picturesque neighborhoods, Bukchon Hanok Village.

Bukchon—or "North Village," owing to its location north of the Cheonggyecheon Stream and Jongno—is Seoul's largest collection of Korean traditional homes, or *hanok*. Traditionally, located as it is between the two palaces, the neighborhood has long been home to Seoul's "old money"—high-ranking officials, royalty and the like.

Throughout most of the Joseon era, Bukchon was a highly exclusive neighborhood—there were no more than 30 villas found here. Towards the end of the Joseon era, however, things began to change dramatically. Social and economic factors led the large estates that previously dominated the neighborhood to be divided up into smaller proper-ties, leading to what you can see now—row upon row of *hanok*, the roof eaves of which seemingly join one another to form a sea of Korean tile roofs. This "urban *hanok*," with its short roof eaves, is believed to have developed in the 1930s. Its development reflects changes in the social environment, where modernization witnessed rural dwellers flocking to the city centers, leading to high population con-centrations in urban areas. Previously, *hanok* homes were built of high-priced materials and designed and constructed by professional woodcrafters. With buildings placed with room to breath, space was rarely an issue. These urban *hanok*, however, were mass-produced, and while the homes maintained a central courtyard as found in traditional *hanok*, they were designed to make the most of limited space.

The result, which you see today, is really quite beautiful—an unbroken line of *hanok* roofs, the eaves almost touching one another, with neighbors sharing the same beautiful walls. Koreans strolling through this area are reminded of a more rustic time in Korean history. The alleyways in particular give off a warm, human feeling. Unlike the West, where roads tend to run straight (unless you live in San Francisco), the alleyways in Bukchon branch off like veins on a leaf—they flow along the hills almost like water. Like Insa-dong Road, which developed alongside a stream flowing into the Cheonggyecheon Stream, the alleyways of Bukchon developed by following the slopes and ridge lines of Mt. Bukhansan. The narrow alleys form a virtual labyrinth, and it's this labyrinth that gives the neighborhood much of its unique charm.

In terms of *feng shui*, Bukchon united the two palaces, Gyeongbokgung and Changdeokgung, which occupy the finest locations in Seoul. It sits on the south side of a mountain slope linking Mt. Bugaksan and Mt. Eungbongsan; accordingly, it was considered a particularly vital and auspicious place to live. It was warm in the winter, had great drainage (a major plus in early cities), and offered spectacular views of Mt. Namsan. Since it provided such a wonderful working and living environment, the neighborhood tended to fill up with the rich and powerful.

Moreover, since the rich and powerful lived in such close proximity to one another, they could exchange information rather easily, allowing them to band together to strengthen and prolong their grip on power. Such was the making of Bukchon. Low ranking officials, on the other hand, tended to congregate in Namchon ("South Village"), located on the slopes of Mt. Namsan, in what are currently Namsan-dong, Pil-dong and Mukjeong-dong. As opposed to Bukchon, where positive *yang* energy was dominant, Namchon was rich in negative *eum* energy. It, too, had good drainage and plenty of underground water.

❋ How to Enjoy Bukchon

To truly enjoy Bukchon, you need to get lost in it.

Many people seem to look for something like a folk village in Bukchon. But it's a big mistake. Bukchon is a place created by layers of time—a very uniquely Korean neighborhood composed of traditional Korean-style houses standing side by side with vivid traces of wear and tear, which have turned into prized cultural assets.

There are several routes leading to Bukchon. The old alleyways of Gahoe-dong, Gye-dong and Wonseo-dong are popular accesses, all graced with dense layers of time but also undergoing noticeable efforts to attain creative evolution.

Horse Rock (Malbawi), reached after a short walk along the old city wall from Waryong-dong, should be the best point to begin our promenade. From the top of Mt. Baegaksan one can have a whole view of Bukchon. With Mt. Baegaksan to the rear, Mt. Inwangsan rises far away on the right side and Mt. Taraksan stretches to the left side to form a natural greenbelt embracing the two palaces and Jongmyo, the royal ancestral shrine of Joseon, with Bukchon nestled between them.

No doubt the imposing high-rise buildings will first come into sight, but it's still a wonderful view. Climbing

down the mountain, the walk continues into the alley between the Vietnamese Embassy and Kyungnam University's Institute of Far Eastern Studies, with the Board of Audit and Inspection to the rear. Past a traditional-style house renovated by a German in his own way and open houses remodeled as a natural dyeing workshop and a tea culture institute, one encounters the first famous cluster of traditional homes at **31 Gahoe-dong**. This section has drawn the greatest public attention from the initial stage of the "Bukchon Traditional Houses Conservation Project." The area indeed retains the original landscape and mood to the highest degree.

The **house of Lee Jun-gu**, built in the late 1930s, looks prominent enough to serve as a geographical landmark. With well-preserved granite outer walls and a French-style pointed roof, the house is named Seoul Municipal Cultural Property Material No. 2. From this house as the cardinal point, a group of genuine Korean-style houses was removed to give way to a large-scale luxury housing complex many years ago. These houses are mostly rented by foreign companies and embassies.

To the southwest is the famed cluster of modern row house-type *hanok* at **31 Gahoe-dong**. Some of these are private houses but many interesting cultural facilities are scattered around this charming neighborhood. They include workshops specializing in folk arts and crafts such as embroidery, rush mat weaving, dressmaking and tea culture. Seoul City provides subsidies to privately-owned homes that are registered as "open houses" used for cultural purposes and opened to visitors for a specific time. The gentle roof lines overlapped with one another, exquisite courtyards and decorative brick walls facing the narrow alleyways characterize these houses standing next to one another.

Passing through this alley and walking southward awhile, one will find Donmi Drugstore, the longtime landmark at the main crossroads, facing Jaedong Primary School on the opposite side. Cross the road here to explore another fascinating section of Bukchon, spread around 11 **Gahoe-dong**.

The area has a number of small museums and houses open for hands-on experience in traditional Korean culture and lifestyle. Seoul City purchased some of the traditional-style houses in this area and renovated them. Then the city government selected resident custodians to run small museums of decorative knots, amulets and needlework. Some houses offer guided tours of interiors and tea culture sessions. A Frenchman bought a house and renovated it to his liking, enhancing the cultural appeal of the neighborhood. Places include the Museum of Korean Buddhist Art, Ojuk Gongbang (02-3676-7519), Otchil Gongbang (02-735-5757) Institute of Korean Royal Cuisine (02-3673-1122~3), Gahoe Museum (02-741-0466) and Maedeup Gongbang (02-3673-2778).

There are two routes leading to the **Bukchon Cultural Center** from Joongang High School. One is a road stretching southward, and the other is a side alley to the east that leads out to the Wonseo-dong road running along the stone wall of Changdeokgung Palace. From here one can return to Bukchon and then soon find the cultural center. One thing that should not be missed here is the **view of Changdeokgung Palace** from the hilly road. Over the stone wall the palace grounds sprawl with the renovated Gyujanggak, the royal library; Seonwonjeon (Hall of Beautiful Origin), the palace shrine of the royal family; and Eokseongnu (Pavilion of Reflections on Past Memories). Beyond these structures is seen the side of the main throne hall, Injeongjeon (Hall of Benevolent Governance).

The **Bukchon Cultural Center** at 105 Gye-dong was originally the house of Min Hyeong-gi, who served as a financial official in the late Joseon period. The house was built in 1921 for his son upon his marriage. His daughter-in-law, Yi Gyu-suk, lived here until 1935. The house was built by palace carpenters copying Yeongyeongdang (House of Flowing Happiness), a Confucian literati-style

mansion within Changdeokgung Palace, where the layout of buildings and gardens shows a certain principle. It was the first hanok in the area bought by Seoul City.

Since it opened on October 29, 2002, the cultural center has operated a public relations hall promoting the history and value of Bukchon, a counseling room providing information and assistance regarding renovation of traditional houses, and a neighbors' lounge. It also offers lectures on such subjects as calligraphy, tea culture, Chinese characters and the pansori epic chants. Workshops on traditional arts and crafts including natural dyeing, black bamboo craft, decorative knots and patchwork are drawing many participants.

❃ Conservation Vs. Development?

The preservation of the neighborhood has proven quite the headache. Of the 2,300 homes in the area, some 900 are *hanok*. In 2001, Seoul Metropolitan Government launched the Bukchon Project, an 84 billion-won project to revitalize the neighborhood's *hanok* culture by registering *hanok* homes, providing support to repair and renovate hanok, and promoting the sale and use of *hanok*.

The project, however, led to some rather unusual side

effects. For starters, it excluded several large swaths of Bukchon, for instance, the western side of Samcheong-dong and the area around the Hyundai Building. In areas excluded from the project, ordinary zoning laws were applied. What this created was a situation where some areas were required to follow strict zoning laws banning buildings of over two stories, while others could build buildings of four stories or more. In the east side of Samcheon-dong, for example, building owners not only had to preserve the exterior of their buildings, but keep their uses the same, too. On the west side, however, builders were free to build large commercial buildings.

Through 2007, some 392 of the area's 924 hanok homes have registered voluntarily with the Bukchon project. Most of those have received support from the government.

One of the trends in the neighborhood is a move towards a) new construction, and b) changes in use. Initially, there was a great interest in repairing existing

homes with a corresponding drop in new construction, but with the recent spike in land prices, new construction has been on the rise. In 2006, some 14 new buildings were built in Bukchon, including *hanok* and non-*hanok*. More noticeable are changes in use. In 2006 and 2007, a combined 33 homes were converted into commercial establishments of some kind—12 became restaurants, five became offices, and 11 were turned into teashops, academies and other businesses.

What all these statistics mean, in the end, is that the atmosphere of Bukchon has been changing. Bukchon was—and is—first and foremost a residential neighborhood. It's a place where people live. Yet over the last couple of years, it has transformed into something of a tourist destination, with a proliferation of coffee shops, tea houses, restaurants, guest houses and wine bars. Given the romance of the neighborhood, this should come as no surprise, and truth be told, it is a rather pleasant experience to sit on a rooftop cafe and sip a glass of wine while taking in the scenery below. Still, it has had a profound effect on the neighborhood's character and identity, and not necessarily a good one. While Bukchon is far from being a folk village, it has become considerably more commercialized and "touristy," much to the chagrin of many of its residents. For the neighborhood to be truly preserved, there first needs to be a recognition that Bukchon is more than simply pretty walls and roofs—it's a living, breathing community with its own unique culture. Should that unique culture disappear, it would be difficult—if not impossible—to get it back. And for Seoul, that would be a tragedy.

仁政門

TOUR * 4
19th Century Royal Residences I

Changdeokgung Palace and
Unhyeongung Palace Residence

This walk will take us to Changdeokgung Palace, a
UNESCO World Heritage Site and possibly the most beautiful of Seoul's palaces, and Unhyeongung Palace, a wonderful example of late-Joseon residential architecture. We
will become acquainted with how Korea's royals lived in
the 19th century, as well as look at the most spectacular of
Korean traditional gardens, the Huwon (Rear Garden) of
Changdeokgung Palace.

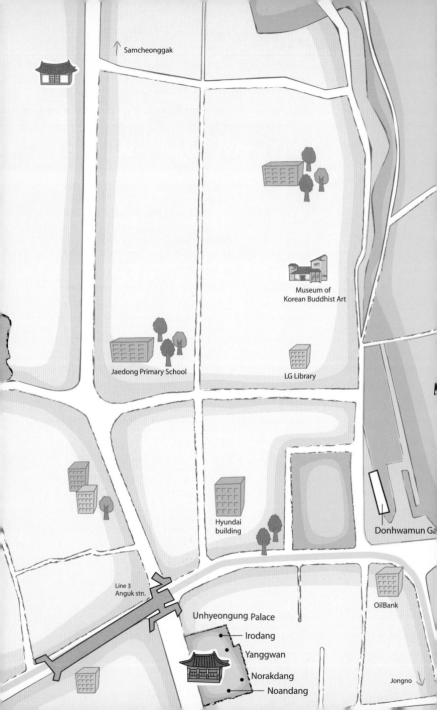

↑ Samcheonggak

Museum of
Korean Buddhist Art

Jaedong Primary School

LG Library

Hyundai
building

Donhwamun Ga

Line 3
Anguk stn.

OilBank

Unhyeongung Palace

Irodang

Yanggwan

Norakdang

Noandang

Jongno →

ndeokjeong
Gwallamjeong
Bando-ji
Yeongyeongdang
Aeryeonji
Juham-nu
won
Buyongjeong
Buyongji
Bullomun
Changdeokgung Palace
Changgyeonggung Palace
njeongjeon Hall
Nakseonjae
Jongmyo

1 ❀ Changdeokgung Palace: An Overview

Changdeokgung Palace was originally built as a royal villa in 1405, during the reign of King Taejong. Most of the major buildings of the palace complex were completed at this time. In 1412, the imposing Donhwamun Gate was built, and in 1463, the complex was greatly expanded when the now famous Huwon (Rear Garden) was more than doubled in size.

Like Seoul's other palaces, Changdeokgung Palace was burnt down during the Japanese invasion of 1592. It was rebuilt in 1610 by then-king Prince Gwanghae as his

palace, but it again burned down when Gwanghae was dethroned in a coup in 1623. In 1647, King Injo began rebuilding the complex, although fire would continue to plague the palace. That being said, from 1610 to the restoration of the Gyeongbokgung Palace in 1872, it served as Seoul's primary royal residence and seat of government.

In 1910, the treaty that made official Japan's annexation of Korea was signed in Changdeokgung Palace's throne room. A major fire in 1917 destroyed many of the buildings, with Gyeongbokgung paying the price—many of the Gyeongbokgung's buildings were torn down and moved them to Changdeokgung, ostensibly to "restore" it. Efforts were also made to alter the palace in ways conducive to japanese aims, such as moving the Seonwonjeon Hall—which contained the portraits of the Joseon kings—to a hidden part of the palace. When Emperor Sunjong—the last of the Joseon kings—died here in 1926, much of the palace fell into disrepair. Instead, the Japanese turned it into a park open to the public, installing exhibition halls and other tourist facilities. Even the Huwon, called by the Japanese the Biwon or "Secret Garden," was significantly altered.

In the 1990s, however, major restoration work was undertaken. Today, Changdeokgung Palace is the only Seoul palace where you can see a real, live royal pleasure garden of the Joseon era.

In 1997, the palace was listed on UNESCO's list of World Cultural Heritage Sites.

❀ Guided Tours

Unless you're willing to spend 15,000 won (subject to change) on the palace's once-a-week "free tour" allowing you to walk around the complex at your own leisure, you need to join a tour group (in Korean, English, Japanese or Chinese) to see the place, and even then, some areas like the Nakseonjae are closed off unless you've joined a special tour for which you need to book a spot.

2❋ Yeongyeongdang

One of the more interesting structures in Changdeokgung Palace is an oddly rustic-looking complex that can be found in the Huwon Garden. This complex, which resembles the handsome yet simple homes of Joseon era country gentry, is **Yeongyeongdang Hall**. The hall was built in the early 19th century, when Crown Prince Hyomyeong was ruling the country in the name of his father, King Sunjo. King Sunjo, who reigned from 1800 to 1834, entrusted Hyomyeong with running state affairs in 1827, when the prince turned 18. The idea behind the complex was to give the young prince a taste of rural gentry life. Unfortunately, the prince died three years later in 1830, and Sunjo would have to run the country until his death in 1834. The complex would continue to grow throughout the years, and would become politically important when King Gojong retreated here after Chinese troops raided Changdeokgung Palace during the Reformists' Coup of 1884. It also served as Emperor

Anchae of Yeongyeongdang

Sunjong's residence following the fire of 1917.

Yeongyeongdang Hall is a beautiful piece of 19th century Joseon-era residential architecture, but unfortunately, it's open only two days a week. If you are lucky enough to visit when it's open, however, you're in for a real treat. The enclosed compound is easily recognized by its overall humility—unlike the other structures of the palace, which are brightly painted, Yeongyeongdang Hall has been left unpainted. If you've seen Korean gentry homes in the countryside, you'll immediately

Front Gate

Seonhyangjae

recognize the building's charms. The compound has three courtyards—an outer courtyard, an eastern courtyard and a western courtyard—and five buildings: a master's quarters, a study, an inner quarters, a kitchen and a pleasure pavilion.

The outer courtyard is what you enter when you pass through the front gate of the compound. Here, you'll find two more gates. The one on the left will take you to the western courtyard, where the womenfolk conducted their business. The one on the right takes you to the eastern courtyard, where men and guests stayed. A couple of notes of interest—the gate to the men's quarters has a raised roof, while the one to the women's quarters does not. The inner gates are positioned in a way that you cannot see into the inner courtyards from outside the main gate, but those inside can see out.

In the eastern courtyard you'll find the master's quarters, study and pavilion. The living quarters, or Sarangchae, consists of a large, open room with a wooden floor (*daecheong*), a closed, floor-heated room (*ondolbang*) and an elevated space where the occupant could relax (*numaru*). The study, or Seonhyangjae, is a particularly unique building, and given the obvious Chinese influence (brick walls, roofed porch), it was probably built in the late 19th century or early 20th century. The bronze-covered porch roof was designed to protect the building, which faces west, from the sun. Behind the study is the Noksujeong Pavilion, which sits on a small hill.

The western courtyard is were you'll find the inner quarters and kitchen. The inner quarters, or Anchae, where the womenfolk would live, also consists of a *daecheong, ondolbang* and *numaru*. It's actually attached to the Sarangchae via an interior passageway, but a stone wall makes it appear to be a separate space altogether.

3❋ Nakseonjae

Nakseonjae was first built in 1847, during the reign of King Heonjong. The name means "Home where people enjoy doing good things." It was built as a residence for King Heonjong's grandmother (Queen Sunwon), himself and Lady Kim, a 14-year-old concubine who managed to capture the heart of the young king.

Unfortunately, King Heonjong and Lady Kim's time of bliss did not last long—the king died in 1849, at the age of 22.

Many queens and princesses breathed their last breaths in this compound, including Empress Sunjeong (died in 1966), Princess Deokhye (the daughter of King Gojong, who died in 1989) and Crown Princess Uimin (born Princess Masako of Nashimoto), the wife of Crown Prince Eun who died in 1989.

Since Nakseonjae was built primarily as a residence for women, the compound has a distinctly feminine touch to it, with very fine designs and woodwork. There are three main buildings—Nakseonjae proper (where the king would sleep), the Sugangjae (where Queen Sunwon slept) and finally the Seokbokheon, where Lady Kim slept. Interestingly, the Seokbokheon was placed in the middle, so Lady Kim could easily tend to both the king and his grandmother. American readers might also find it of interest that Julia Mullock, the American wife of Korea's last crown prince, lived in the Seokboheon.

The Nakseonjae and Seokbokheon are unpainted, while the Sugangjae is brightly painted.

You'll notice quite a few symbols of profundity throughout the complex. For example, the railings of the Seokbokheon feature carvings of calabashes, which were seen as a symbol of fertility. On the rear gate to the complex, a stone circular portal, you'll find a painting of grapes, another sign of fertility. In back, there is an outstanding example of Korean palace garden architecture, with a terraced garden topped by three pavilions that offer outstanding views of the surroundings.

4❋ Huwon

The **Huwon,** or **Rear Garden,** is sometimes referred to as the Biwon (Secret Garden), Geumwon (Forbidden Garden) or Bukwon (North Garden). The landscaping on the garden dates back to the 15th century, and is considered the epitome of Korean traditional garden design.

There are three main areas in the Huwon—the Buyongji Pond area, the Aeryeonji Pond area and Bandoji Pond area. At one time, there were over 100 pavilions in the Huwon, but now, there are only 18.

Korean gardens seek to remain as close to nature as possible. The key is to blend with and take advantage of the landscape. For Korean garden designers, nature—with its plethora of hills, streams and woods, the natural surrounding—was enough. Any additional elements, such as the ponds and pavilions of the Huwon, are added to enhance the natural landscape.

The best-known area of the Huwon is the **Buyongji Pond.** Although the garden centers on an artificial pond, all

 its elements harmonize with one another to form a natural and organic whole. The pond, which has a small island in the middle, is surrounded by a number of beautiful pavilions, each one offering different views of the garden. The most beautiful of these is the **Buyongjeong Pavilion**, which sits on the southern side of the pond. With its beautiful design and superb use of location and scale, Buyongjeong Pavilion is both a thing of beauty in and of itself and an integral part of the surroundings. **Juham-nu Pavilion**, once a royal library and academic institute, sits high atop a terraced platform, with beautiful views of the grounds below.

The pond is a traditionally East Asian representation of the cosmos, with the square pond representing Earth and the round island in the middle representing the heavens.

This is a place where, time permitting, you could spend hour upon hour simply gazing at the landscape and never get bored.

Just past the Buyongji Pond is another pond, the **Aeryeonji Pond**, which you enter by passing through a small stone gate—the **Bullomun Gate**—whose name promises eternal youth. The gate is carved from a single piece of granite. In autumn, the leaves of the maple trees around Aeryeonji Pond are quite striking as they turn bright red. It's also here you'll find the Yeongyeongdang.

The third area, the **Bandoji Pond** area, is much quieter than the rest of the garden due to it being somewhat removed from the other two sections. The highlight here is the **Gwallamjeong Pavilion**, built during the reign of King Gojong, with its unique fan-like design. The ornate **Jondeokjeong Pavilion**, with its octagonal roof, is also worth checking out while you're here.

Still further is the **Ongnyucheon,** an artificial stream amidst a rock valley surrounded by five pavilions. Particularly impressive is how, despite the stream being artificial, it's very difficult to find a human touch anywhere. One of the pavilions, the **Cheonguijeong Pavilion,** has a thatched roof and is surrounded by a small rice paddy. This is where the king would practice rice farming, to allow him to grow better acquainted with the lives of the common people.

5❀ Unhyeongung Palace Residence

Unhyeongung Palace was not really a "palace," per se, although King Gojong did live there until the age of 12 (1863), when he ascended the throne and moved to Changdeokgung Palace. The residence is famous as the home of Heungseon Daewongun, the conservative prince regent who was the effective ruler of Korea during Gojong's minority and for a good time afterwards.

The palace, built between 1863 and 1873, was a typical upper-class Korean home until Gojong took the throne and the residence was greatly expanded. During Heungseon Daewongun's decade-long regency, Unhyeongung Palace was Korea's real seat of power and the center of much drama and intrigue as Joseon Korea attempted to modern-

ize and reform in the face of imperial threats from overseas.

Unlike the real palaces, don't expect to see colorfully painted buildings and imposing throne rooms. Here, you're treated to classic residential architecture of the late Joseon era, characterized by the rustic Confucian modesty so typical of the period. Particularly beautiful are the intricate designs on the "flower wall" (*kkot dam*) in the front courtyard.

❀ Noandang

The first major structure you come to at Unhyeongung Palace is the **Noandang Hall**. The Noandang Hall was the men's quarters and the residence of Heungseon Daewongun. Unlike most other residential buildings of its time, it sits on a stone platform three bricks high. It's a rather pleasant structure, shaped in a T, with foldaway doors and windows that let the breeze in to bring comfort in the hot Korean summer. You'll also note the wood and copper awnings attached to the roof eaves—you can find these awnings on other buildings at Unhyeongung Palace as well.

The signboard is also worth noting, as it's a composition of works produced by the great Korean calligraphy master Kim Jeong-hui (1786–1856).

✦ Norakdang and Irodang

The **Norakdang** is the main chamber of the palace complex. It was here that King Gojong—then 15 years of age—married the 16-year-old Queen Myeongseong in 1866. Next door is the **Irodang**, the women's quarters, where Queen Myeongseong learned how to behave like a queen. Like the Noandang, it sits on a high stone platform, something not seen in other private homes. Although it has plenty of windows, it doesn't have any doors, and is instead entered via a corridor that connects it with the Norakdang. Particularly beautiful is the hall's central courtyard.

✦ Unhyeongung Yanggwan

The Neo-Baroque **Unhyeongung Yanggwan** ("Western-style Hall of the Unhyeongung Palace") is one of the most beautiful examples of early modern architecture in Seoul. The imposing white building was built in 1912 as the home of Yi Jun-yong, the grandson of Heungseon Daewongun. When he died, the building was taken over by Prince Yi Wu, who was killed when the Americans dropped the atomic bomb on Hiroshima in 1945. It's now an office

belonging to Duksung Women's University's continuing education program.

The garden area around the Yanggwan, which is actually separate from the Unhyeongung Palace itself and approached via a gate just past the palace complex, is a pleasant place to stroll about. There's a small Western/Japanese style pavilion left over from the colonial period as well.

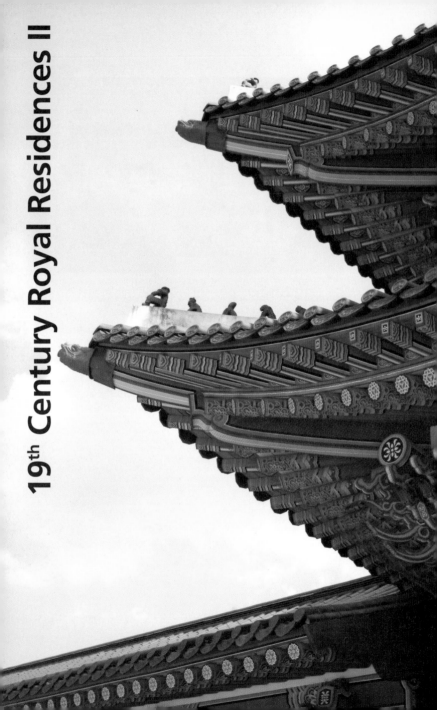

19th Century Royal Residences II

TOUR * 5
19th Century Royal Residences II

Geoncheonggung Royal Residence and Chilgung Shrine

Gyeongbokgung Palace is one of Seoul's most visited tourist attractions and a powerful symbol of Korea's proud royal history. The most important of the Joseon Dynasty's royal residences, it served for centuries as the nation's center of power. In fact, it still does—while the palace itself may now be vacant, just in back of it is Cheong Wa Dae, the mansion of the Republic of Korea's president. Most tours of the palace focus on the grander structures at the southern end of the complex. This tour, however, will visit some of the lesser appreciated structures to the north end of the palace, including the historic Geoncheonggung Residence and Jibokjae Hall. It will also visit the Chilgung ("Seven Shrine"), where memorial shrines to seven royal concubines are located.

Buam-dong ↗

6 Chilgung

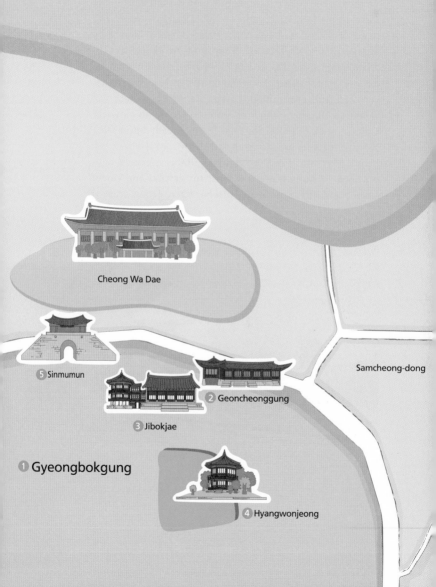

Bugak Mountain

Cheong Wa Dae

Samcheong-dong

5 Sinmumun

2 Geoncheonggung

3 Jibokjae

1 Gyeongbokgung

4 Hyangwonjeong

1❋ Gyeongbokgung Palace: An Overview

As the official palace, **Gyeongbokgung** is symbolically the most important of Joseon (1392–1910) palaces. The name of the palace means "the Palace Greatly Blessed by Heaven" or "Palace of Resplendent Happiness." "Sambong" Jeong Do-jeon (1337–1398), the prime minister who had assisted the founding of the Joseon dynasty, selected and recommended the name "Gyeongbok" (Chinese: Jingfu), which is adopted from the classical Chinese book of Odes, Shi Jing: "I am already intoxicated by alcohol and my stomach is full of moral virtue (德 deok). May your Lordship enjoy 10,000 resplendent happinesses." The passage is a wish for eternal enjoyment from the cultivation of moral character. Jeong created

this name to stress the need for morality as well as to eulogize the new state.

Gyeongbokgung Palace was completed in 1395, three years after the Joseon Dynasty was founded by the general Yi Seong-gye, when the capital of the newly founded dynasty moved from Gaekyeong (modern day Kaesong in North Korea) to Seoul (then known as Hanyang). With Mt. Baegaksan (342.4m) to its rear and Mt. Mokmyeoksan (now called Mt. Namsan) in the fore-ground, the site of Gyeongbokgung was deemed auspi-cious according to the traditional practice of geomancy. In front of Gwanghwamun Gate, the main entrance to the palace, ran Yukjo-geori (Street of Six Ministries, today's Sejongno), home to major government offices. Along the central axis upon which Gwanghwamun Gate stood was the nucleus of the palace, including the throne hall, recep-tion hall and king's residence.

The government ministry district and main buildings of Gyeongbokgung formed the heart of the capital city of Seoul and represented the sovereignty of the Joseon Dynasty. After all the palaces in the capital were razed during the Japanese invasions of 1592–1598, Changdeokgung, a detached palace, was rebuilt and served as the main palace. Gyeongbokgung was left derelict for the next 250 years. It was finally reconstructed in 1868 by the order of the Prince Regent. The palace the Prince Regent created was markedly different from the original. Some 330 buildings were built on a site of over 40 hectares and constituted a small city. The architectural principles of ancient China were harmoniously incorpo-rated into both the tradition and the appearance of the Joseon royal court. Gyeongbokgung was largely torn down during the Japanese occupation. Some 85% of the restored buildings was dismantled, Gwanghwamun Gate was removed, and an enormous building housing the Japanese Government-General was constructed in front of the main sector of the palace. An effort to fully restore

Gyeongbokgung Palace to its former glory has been ongoing since 1990. The colonial Government-General building was removed, and Heungnyemun Gate was restored to its original state. The royal quarters and the East Palace for the crown prince were also restored to their original state.

2❀ Geoncheonggung Royal Residence

Geoncheonggung ("Clear Sky Palace") was built in 1873 (the 10th year of King Gojong), five years after Gyeongbokgung was rebuilt. Located in a secluded place in the northernmost part of the palace, it was built for the king and the queen to enjoy peace and quiet. A large pond called Hyangwonji was created nearby, with a pavilion at the center. The residence followed the architecture of a typical scholar's residence, except for a few ornate decorations. Jangandang Hall ("Long Peace Hall") for the king, Gonnyeonghap Hall ("Peaceful Lord Hall") for the queen and Gwanmungak Library behind Jangandang are laid out to copy the men's quarters, women's quarters and the library of the typical literati's residence. The surrounding brick walls are decorated with beautiful flower patterns.

King Gojong liked the residence so much that he stayed

there frequently with his queen. When the king and the queen did not reside in these quarters, portraits of preceding kings were housed there. In contrast to the intended purpose of relaxation, this residence was an arena of political turmoil toward the end of the Joseon Dynasty. This was where King Gojong received ministers from the United States, Great Britain and Russia to resolve a variety of political issues. During these years of upheaval, a Russian architect rebuilt Gwanmungak Library as a two-story brick edifice. The first electric lights in the palace were installed here. In 1895, a group of ruffians raided this residence and slaughtered Queen Myeongseong, King Gojong's wife. She died in Okhoru, the high veranda of Gonnyeonghap.

The original Geoncheonggung was torn down during the Japanese occupation period—what you see now is a recently completed restoration.

3❋ Hyeopgildang, Jibokjae and Parujeong

Not far from Geoncheonggung is a collection of three unique buildings. These three palace buildings (from east to west) are **Hyeopgildang**, **Jibokjae** and **Parujeong** (frequently referred to collectively as the Jibokjae). They were originally built in the precincts of Changdeokgung, but were moved to Gyeongbokgung in 1888 when King Gojong relocated his official residence there. King Gojong used the buildings as an art hall in which to enshrine royal portraits, a library and an audience hall for the reception

of foreign envoys. Records show that in 1893 the king granted five audiences to foreign envoys from Great Britain, Japan and Austria.

The architectural style of Jibokjae differs

significantly from that of other palace buildings, clearly displaying the influence of Chinese architecture, which at that time was regarded as "modern" by Korean builders.

4⊛ Pavilion of Far-Reaching Fragrance: Hyangwonjeong

When Geoncheonggung Residence was built, King Gojong redesigned the palace's back garden. An artificial islet was created in the middle of the pond, on which a hexagonal pavilion was built with the name **Hyangwonjeong**, meaning the "Pavilion of Far-Reaching Fragrance" The bridge across the pond was named Chwihyanggyo, meaning "intoxicated with fragrance."

In 1873, when King Gojong built Geoncheonggung, he

had a pond dug to the south, with an islet created in the middle. A two-tier hexagonal pavilion, built on the islet, was named Hyangwonjeong and the wooden bridge leading to it was called Chwihyanggyo

Chwihyanggyo Bridge was the longest wooden bridge constructed on a pond during the Joseon Dynasty. At present, the wooden bridge from the south provides access to the islet, but the bridge was originally on the north side to be reached from Geoncheonggung. In 1953, the bridge was moved to the south side of the pond. The sources of the pond are underground water and a spring coming down from the mountain at the back of the palace. The water eventually flows into the pond where Gyeonghoeru Pavilion stands.

5❋ North Gate of Gyeongbokgung: Sinmumun

The **North Gate** was erected after the northern wall of the palace was constructed. In 1475 (the sixth year of King Seongjong), this gate obtained the name Sinmumun. Few people used the north gate, except when civil servants participated in rare gatherings to pledge alliance at a site located near the gate. During King Yeongjo's reign (1724–1776), when ancestral memorial services were held

for the king's mother, Sukbin, the gate was used as a path to Yuksanggung (later Chilgung), the shrine housing her memorial tablet. Sukbin (family name Choe) was a concubine of King Sukjong and King Yeongjo's mother. Sinmumun is on the same scale as Geonchunmun— the current gate was erected when Gyeongbokgung was rebuilt in 1865.

6❋ Seven Shrines: Chilgung

Yuksanggung is the shrine for Concubine Choe, who was one of the consorts of King Sukjong and also the mother of King Yeongjo. The shrine was named Sukbinmyo when it was built in the first year of the reign of King Yeongjo (1725) and renamed Yuksanggung in the 20th year of King Yeongjo with the intention to give higher status to it. It was burnt down in the 19th year of King Gojong (1882) but rebuilt the next year. It's also called "**Chilgung**," which means "Seven shrines," because seven shrines previously located in other regions were compounded here in 1908. The seven shrines—Yuksanggung, Jeogyeonggung, Daebingung, Yeonugung, Seonhuigung, Gyeongugung, and Deogangung— are dedicated to the tablets of seven mothers of kings who had never officially become queens. To the left of Yuksanggung, surrounded by a small wall, four respective shrines stand facing each other. The places for memorial rites are located in front of the shrines. In typical Korean garden style, the yard around the shrines displays a neat and simple beauty.

To visit the Chilgung, you must first make a reservation through the presidential mansion of Cheong Wa Dae—see the Cheong Wa Dae homepage (www.president.go.kr) for more details.

Around Mysterious
Mt. Inwangsan

TOUR *6
Around Mysterious Mt. Inwangsan

The Udae Neighborhood

In the old days, the area around Mt. Inwangsan, in the northwest part of Seoul, used to be called Udae. The Udae neighborhood is one of Seoul's most picturesque areas, in large part thanks to Mt. Inwangsan itself. Mt. Inwangsan (338m), with its spectacular granite cliff faces and unusual rock formations, used to be called the "White Tiger Mountain" during the Joseon era, and was considered one of Seoul's "guardian mountains." You won't find any real tigers up here anymore, sadly, but you will find an atmosphere unlike anywhere else in Seoul. The mountain is famous for its *pungsu* (or Chinese, *feng shui*), or geomantic properties, and not surprisingly, it is a favorite congregating point for Seoul's shaman community. Along its slopes you'll find one of the most important shrines in Korean shamanism, the Guksadang, and the famous Seon Rock, another noted shamanist site.

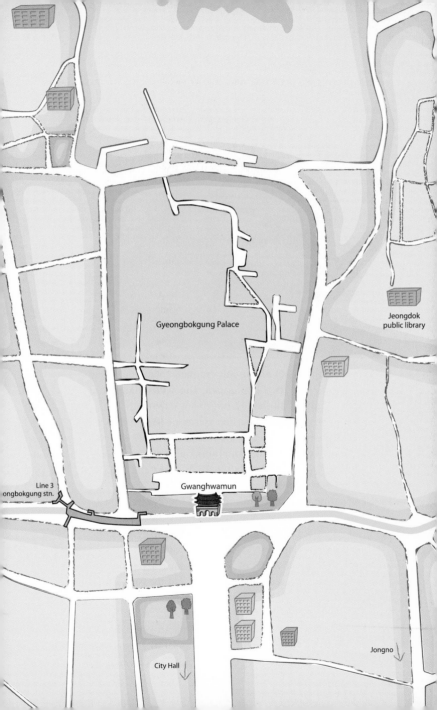

Gyeongbokgung Palace

Jeongdok
public library

Line 3
ongbokgung stn.

Gwanghwamun

City Hall

Jongno

1❈ Guksadang National Ritual Shrine

Located on the slopes of Mt. Inhwangsan, a mountain long regarded as holy by shamanists, the **Guksadang** is a shamanist prayer hall that enshrines not only the portraits of shamanist gods, but also the spirits of King Taejo (r. 1329–1398)—the founder of the Joseon kingdom—and the Venerable Muhak Jacho, a high-ranking Buddhist monk who served as the king's advisor. Both Taejo and Muhak came to be considered Buddhist gods.

The shrine used to be located atop Mt. Namsan (near where N Seoul Tower is now), but was moved to Mt. Inhwangsan in 1925. The move was sparked by the construction by the Japanese colonial authorities of a massive Shinto shrine on the slopes of Mt. Namsan. The Japanese, it would appear, believed it inappropriate that the Guksadang should occupy a higher position than the new imperial Japanese shrine.

Today, the shrine is a colorful but simple structure. Inside the hall, you can find the portraits of shamanist gods, along with food offerings given by the faithful, who come here in

Photograph courtesy of Prof. David Mason

droves from all over the country, particular in the first lunar month. While many kinds of shamanist ceremonies, or *gut*, are held in the hall, there is no "shaman in residence," so to speak. Instead, the keeper of the shrine rents it out to shamans who ask. Usually, some three or four ceremonies are held here a day, although more might be held in the third and tenth months of the lunar calendar. On the last lunar month, there are hardly any *gut* performed.

Every two years, the shrine keeper will perform the *maji*, a fantastic shamanist ceremony. This is probably the best time to come to the shrine. The ceremony takes place on a carefully selected day in the 11th lunar month.

❀ Gut

A *gut* is a Korean shamanist ritual. These rituals are usually performed by *mudang*, or shamans.

Shamanism is a folk religion centered on a belief in good and evil spirits who can only be influenced by shamans. The shaman is a professional spiritual mediator who performs rites. In Korean, *mudang* usually refers to female shamans, while male shamans are called *baksu madang*.

The *gut* is essentially a sacrifice to the spirits. They can be colorful affairs, with the shaman doing much singing and dancing in colorful costumes. It's the *mudang*'s role to mediate between the believers and the spirits to whom

Photograph courtesy of Prof. David Mason

they pray. Oft times, the *mudang* will go into a trance as she performs the ritual.

Gut take many different forms. Some are held to pray for success in a new business venture. Some are held to pray for recovery from illness. Still others are to pray for happiness in the afterlife. Regional differences add to the variety.

Like Mongolia and Manchuria, Korea has a long history of shamanism, a legacy of the Central Asian roots of the Korean people. Unfortunately, recent history has not been kind to the shaman. During the Joseon era, *mudang* were placed in the lowest of Korea's social classes. Shamans experienced further repression at the hands of the Japanese colonial authorities, who viewed shamanism as a dangerous expression of Korean cultural identity. The cruelest cut, however, came following Liberation, when post-independence rulers viewed shamanism as superstition and a shameful relic of the past. Shamans were discouraged from holding *gut*, especially in front of foreign eyes. Meanwhile, modernization and Westernization reduced Koreans' interest in shamanism, although it continued to play a part in their lives.

Recently, however, there has been renewed interest in Korea's shamanist tradition. This has in large part been fueled by Korea's rapid economic growth and the accompanying surge in nationalism. As Korea's place in the world grows, and society grows more chaotic, Koreans have begun to rediscover their traditional culture and started turning to the spiritual ways of old for solace.

2 ❈ Seon Rock (Zen Rock)

A short hike from Guksadang is **Seonbawi** (Zen Rock), a large, almost prehistoric-looking rock so-called because it resembles a robed Buddhist monk in meditation. Some say the rock bears the likeness of King Taejo and Venerable Muhak. Regardless of whom or what it resembles, the rock was (and still is) a favorite place for women to pray for sons.

Since the Guksadang was moved to the spot below Seonbawi, the rock has been the object of veneration for ages. There is a small shrine in front of the rock where devotees pray and light candles. The rock also provides an outstanding view of downtown Seoul. It's breathtaking.

There is also an interesting story related to Seonbawi.

When the city walls to protect the royal capital were being built during the reign of King Taejo, there was a good deal of debate whether or not the rock should be included within the city walls. Venerable Muhak lobbied for its inclusion within the walls. Another close advisor of the king, the Confucian scholar "Sambong" Jeong Dojeon (1342–1398), lobbied for its exclusion, believing that if it were included within the walls, Buddhism would flourish over Confucianism. Jeong won the day, and the rock was left outside the walls. Accordingly, Buddhism's fortune in the new kingdom began to wane as the religion took a back seat to Confucianism.

At any rate, there can be no denying the mystical power of Mt. Inwangsan, with its bizarre, almost surreal rock formations and dramatic granite cliffs. When you climb up here, you really do feel as if you've entered another world, far from the hustle and bustle of the city below. It's no wonder so many shamanists congregate here.

3❋ Hwanghakjeong Archery Range

The **Hwanghakjeong Pavilion** was once a royal archery ground. According to the English signboard, it was built in 1898 "to reinvigorate the martial art of archery, which had weakened in Seoul after the Military Revolution of 1884." Even today, the area is used as an archery club, where Seoulites can learn the art of traditional Korean archery.

Hwanghakjeong was erected as an archery pavilion by royal order to the north of Hoesangjeon in Gyeonghuigung Palace in 1898, during the reign of King Gojong. It was moved to its present site in 1922. The spot was originally the site of another archery range, the Deunggwajeong, one of Seoul's five archery grounds during the Joseon period. It is the only Daehan Empire-era (1897–1910) archery range to survive, and archery contests are held here even today. The other four were Deungnyongjeong in Ok-dong, Ullyongjeong in Samcheong-dong, Daesongjeong in Sajik-dong, and Pungsojeong in Nusang-dong.

Just past the archery club is a shrine to Dangun, the mythical founder of the Korean nation, and Sajik Park.

4⊛ Sajikdan

One of the more important roles played by the Joseon kings was to conduct regular rites that were to ensure the peace and prosperity of the kingdom.

One of the most significant of these rites was the Sajikdaeje, a religious service to two gods, Sasin (the god of earth) and Jiksin (the god of the harvest). The rite was a prayer for peace and a bountiful harvest.

The rite dates back to the Three Kingdoms Period, but was greatly expanded during the Joseon era, when Confucianism became the ruling state ideology. It was, in fact, one of the two most important rites of the year, along with the Jongmyoje rite (held to honor the ancestors of the royal family).

The Sajikdaeje featured processions, sacrificial offerings, special attire, and music and dance. Over the years, the precise elements of the rite would change slightly until 1908, when the royal family stopped conducting the rite under Japanese pressure.

In 1988, however, the rite was revived in time for the Seoul Summer Olympic games. Unlike the old days, when the rite would be held three times a year (spring, autumn and winter), it is now held once a year, on Gaecheonjeol, or National Foundation Day (Oct 3).

The rites were held at the **Sajikdan**, an altar located in

what is today Sajik Park. Unfortunately, much of the altar facility has been lost over time. Two stone altars do remain, however—the altar to the east is to honor the god of earth, Sasin, while the one to the west honors the god of the harvest, Jiksin.

◈ Main Gate to the Sajikdan

Of architectural interest, however, is the main gate to the Sajikdan, the **Sajikdan Jeongmun**. Registered as Treasure No. 177, the gate burnt down during the Japanese invasion of 1592, but was rebuilt in 1720. It is a wonderful example of mid-Joseon-era wooden architecture.

5◈ Pirundae Rock

Pirundae Rock, hidden away just behind Paiwha Girl's High School, was the site of Joseon scholar Baeksa Yi Hang-bok's home. Pirun, in fact, was Yi's pen name. The word "Pirundae" is written vertically on the left side of the cliff. In the center are a few lines of poetry, while on the right are the names of nine people.

Yi Hang-bok spent time as a royal secretary and was a well-respected civil servant. The poem in the middle was written in 1889 by one of his descendants, Yi Yu-won, and describes his feeling upon entering the place. The names on the right are presumed to be the people who were involved in the construction of Yi's home. The "Pirundae" characters are believed to have been written by Yi Yu-won as well, while the name list is believed to have been written in 1813 or 1873. The poem is considered a good source for studying the calligraphic penmanship style of the day and gives a good idea about what kind of person Yi Hang-bok was.

"A descendent visits the home where his grandfather used to live,
White clouds absorbed into the green pines and rock face.
Despite the many years, the customs of old have not gone,
The look of the elders is just the same as before."

6＊ Paiwha Girls' High School

Paiwha Girls' High School was founded as the Carolina Hakdang in 1898 by Texas-born missionary Josephine Eaton Peel Campbell of the American Southern Methodist Episcopal Mission. It became the Paiwha Hakdang in 1910, the Paiwha Higher Normal School in 1925 and finally Paiwha Girls High School in 1938. It is most famous for being the alma mater of Yuk Young-soo, the assassinated First Lady of Park Chung-hee.

Paiwha Girls' High School has a number of handsome red-brick buildings from the old days. The dignified Main Hall, for instance, dates from the early colonial period. The most notable of the school's buildings, however, is the **Multi-Purpose Hall**, or *saenghwalgwan*, now a registered cultural property. The Multi-Purpose Hall was originally used as a residence for the missionaries, but since 1971 it has been used as a meeting hall for the school's alumni association. The building preserves the architectural characteristics of homes of American missionaries of the early 20th century. In fact, if you ignore the Korean-style roof

tiles, you'd think you were looking at an ordinary, two-story American red-brick home. Note the beautiful second-floor veranda. The school also provides some nice views over downtown Seoul.

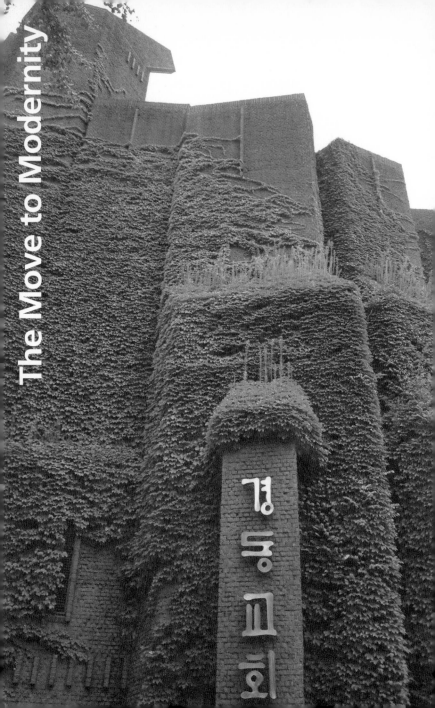

The Move to Modernity

TOUR* 6
The Move to Modernity

Tower Hotel to Dongdaemun

As Korea moved past the ravages of the Korean War, Korean architects began to experiment with new designs made possible by developments in technology. The development of concrete, for instance, opened the way for new and exciting architectural forms. In France, figures like Le Corbusier were revolutionizing the world with futuristic architectural designs. These trends would be felt in Korea, too, with men like Kim Swoo-geun and Kim Chung-up receiving worldwide acclaim for their vision and artistry.

Korean modern architects faced a number of different challenges. One, of course, was Korea's relative poverty in the post-war era, when resources were tight and architectural priorities were focused more on the utilitarian than the ambitious. Technological constraints restricted what Korean architects could do. For instance, Kim Chung-up was forced to change the original design of his beautifully futuristic Seo Gynecology Clinic due to lack of materials and poor local construction technology. Perhaps the biggest challenge for local architects, however, was how to harmonize Korea's proud architectural traditions with the new possibilities offered by technological development. In this walk, we'll see how various architects met these challenges on their way to producing a truly Korean modern architecture.

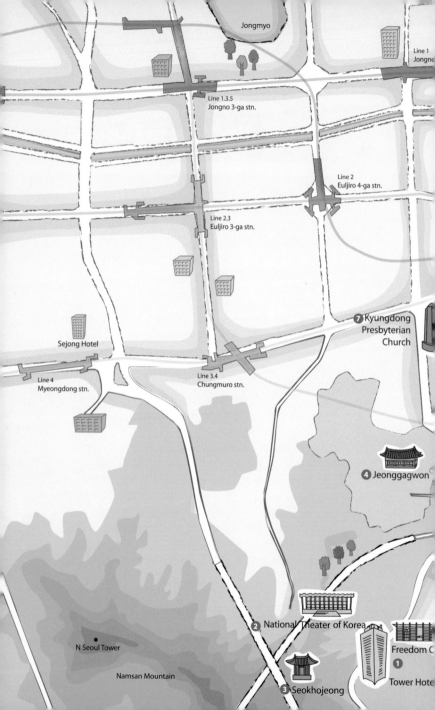

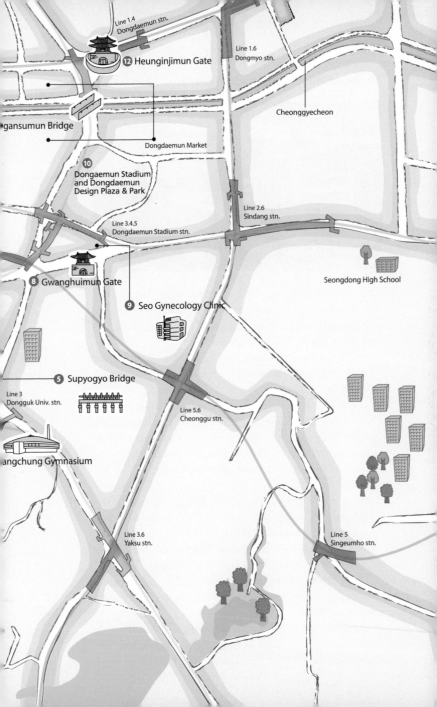

Line 1.4
Dongdaemun stn.

⑫ Heunginjimun Gate

Line 1.6
Dongmyo stn.

Cheonggyecheon

gansumun Bridge

Dongdaemun Market

⑩ Dongaemun Stadium
and Dongdaemun
Design Plaza & Park

Line 2.6
Sindang stn.

Line 3.4.5
Dongdaemun Stadium stn.

Seongdong High School

⑧ Gwanghuimun Gate

⑨ Seo Gynecology Clinic

⑤ Supyogyo Bridge

Line 3
Dongguk Univ. stn.

Line 5.6
Cheonggu stn.

angchung Gymnasium

Line 3.6
Yaksu stn.

Line 5
Singeumho stn.

1 Tower Hotel and Freedom Center

The **Tower Hotel** and the **Freedom Center**, designed by Kim Swoo-geun, were built between 1962 and 1965 as one big monument to anti-communism following the 1959 meeting of the very colorful Asian People's National Anti-Communist League (later the World Anti-Communist League and now the World League for Freedom and Democracy) in Seoul.

The tower was originally conceived as a monument to the nations that fought under the UN flag during the Korean War—it has 17 floors, one for each participating nation, including South Korea. The Freedom Center, meanwhile, was an anti-communist education center.

In 1969, the tower was converted into a hotel. In early 2007, it was sold and is currently undergoing renovation. The Freedom Center, meanwhile, serves as the headquarters of the Korea Freedom League, the Korean branch of the World League for Freedom and Democracy. Nowadays, however, it's probably better known as a wedding hall.

Like a lot of modern contemporary buildings designed in the 60s, the Tower Hotel and Freedom Center use exposed concrete surfaces.

Sadly, Korea's old city walls were partially torn down to build the complex—some of its stones were actually used in the construction of the Freedom Center. Excavation work has turned up traces of the old walls, and restoration work has begun.

❁ Kim Swoo-geun

Kim Swoo-geun (1931-1986) was one of the fathers of Korean modern architecture and probably Korea's most internationally recognized architect. Before passing away at the young age of 55 from liver cancer, he had elevated architecture in Korea from a trade into an art form. He strove to take Korean traditional architectural ideas of space and environment and incorporate them into modern architecture. In many of his creations, space and structures flow together naturally as they do in traditional Korean architecture. In an interview with U.S. magazine TIME, he summed up his architectural philosophy thusly:

"My home is the womb. The womb's home is the mother, the mother's home is the house and the house's home is the environment. It's wrong to think of a home as just a residence. It's the environment. The environment becomes space philosophically, and space is the home of the home's home."

His legacy lives on with the SPACE Group, the architectural firm he founded in 1960.

His major works include the Hilltop Bar of the Walker Hill Hotel (1961), the Freedom Center (1963), the SPACE office (1971), Masan Yangdeok Catholic Church (1977), Kyungdong Presbyterian Church (1980), Olympic Stadium (1984) and Seoul District Court Complex (1986). In 1966, he began publishing SPACE, an architecture magazine, and his 1977, he opened a small theater, "SPACE Love," which held regular performances of poetry, music, drama and dance as well as art exhibitions.

A great architect who worked endlessly toward the rebirth of Korea's culture and art scene, Kim was the recipient of many awards, both from Korea and overseas.

2❋ National Theater of Korea

The **National Theater of Korea** has bounced around quite a bit over its history—it began its life in the occupation era as the Bumingwan on Sejong-no (now the Seoul Municipal Assembly Building) before moving to Myeong-dong. In 1973, it moved to its present home on Mt. Namsan.

The current building was designed by Yi Hi-tae, who along with Kim Swoo-geun and Kim Chung-up was part of that first generation of post-Liberation Korean architects, and constructed between 1968 and 1973. It's been considerably renovated and expanded since then, but the basic structure of the Main Theater remains the same.

In the 1960s, Korean architects tried to tackle the question of how to merge modernity with tradition. The National Theater of Korea reflects this. Yi took the fundamentals of Korean traditional architecture—base, middle and roof—and expressed it in concrete. You can also see the numerous Korean traditional motifs, such as the base pillars, columns and steps leading to an elevated first level. You can find something similar in the Gyeongju National Museum, which was also designed by Yi.

Since 2000, several smaller theaters have been added. The main theater, Hae ("Sun"), has 1,522 seats. The small hall, Dal ("Moon"), has 454 seats, while the experimental studio stage, Byeol ("Star"), has 100 seats. There's also an open air theater that can hold 600.

3❋ Seokhojeong

If you head up Mt. Namsan from in back of the National Theater of Korea's Byeol Theater, you come to the

Seokhojeong.

There's a sign that says "Seupsamueon," which means, "Keep silent so the archer can concentrate."

The Seokhojeong is, along with the Hwanghakjeong (see p100), one of Korea's oldest archery ranges. But while the Hwanghakjeong was a royal archery range, the Seokhojeong was for public use.

The Seokhojeong has a very long history, so it's not exactly known when it was built and by whom, but we do know that the mountain slope behind the Jangchungdan Park had been used as an archery site for quite some time. In the first year of the Daehan Empire (1897), however, the three pavilions that were up there were merged into one, which was named the Seokhojeong.

The term "Seokho" appears to come from ancient Chinese history. It's believed to mean, "Concentrate completely and fire an arrow."

Differences between Korean and Western archery

	Korean	Western
Target	2 x 2.67 m	80 – 120 cm, depending on distance
Distance	145 m	30 – 90 m
Arrow	The head is rounded and bounced off the target.	The head is sharp and pierces the target.
Score	Arrow must hit only the target.	Arrow must hit the circular target, with score determined by how close to the center.

4※ Jeonggagwon (formerly the Sungjeongjeon Hall) of Dongguk University

The **Sungjeongjeon Hall** (Seoul Tangible Cultural Property No. 20), built in the 10th year of Prince Gwanghae (1617), was originally the throne hall of the Gyeonghuigung Palace. It managed to avoid a major fire in 1829, thereby retaining its original shape, but in 1926 it was sold to Jogyesa

Temple and moved. It now stands on the campus of Dongguk University.

The building is built on a double-layer stone foundation, and measures five *kan* (the distance between columns) across and four deep. It has a typical *palgakjibung*-style (a.k.a. hipped and gabled) roof. Three flights of steps descend from the hall, and in the middle of the steps is a stone slab on which is carved a pair of phoenixes. The roof of the building is decorated with gargoyles.

The foundation stones are circular, while the structure is supported by an inner and outer row of columns. In the throne area now stands a Buddhist platform.

5✱ Supyogyo Bridge

The **Supyogyo Bridge** (Seoul Tangible Cultural Property No. 18), a stone bridge, was one of the bridges constructed over the Cheonggyecheon in Supyo-dong in 1406. Construction was completed in 1420. At the time, there was a horse market at the site, so the bridge was called the Majeon-gyo (Horse Market Bridge), but after a watermark was established in 1441 to read the water level of the Cheonggyecheon, it was renamed the Supyogyo

(Watermark Bridge). The watermark was placed on a stone pillar near the bridge in 1760, when the bridge was being repaired. The marks, which indicate four levels, were a measure to prevent flooding. Designated Treasure No. 838, the stone watermark is now in the King Sejong Museum in Hongneung.

The bridge played an important role not just as a means of connection but as a flood prevention device, so in the 36th year of King Yeongjo (1724–1776) a government office was set up at the east end of the bridge to observe water levels.

It's believed from the writing on the bridge that it was reconstructed in 1767–1768.

When work began on covering up the Cheonggyecheon in 1959, the bridge was moved to Hongjedong and then later to Jangchungdan Park in 1965. The bridge is 27.5m long, 7.5m wide and made of granite. Supyogyo Bridge consists in stone slabs placed on long square beams resting over hexagonal bridge columns. The pillars of the bridge are at an angle so they meet less resistance from the flowing water. The bridge's railings are inscribed with images of lotus blossoms and lotus leaves.

6● Jangchung Gymnasium

When it was first designed, the **Jangchung Gymnasium** was supposed to have a shell of reinforced concrete, but it ended up being a steel-frame construction. The stadium, designed by Kim Jeong-su and opened in 1963, was Korea's first large-scale structure capable of holding 10,000 people. In the 1960s, Korean architects made many technical attempts to create large-scale spaces using structure and materials. Steel and prefabrication, with its modern touch, and steel-frame construction came into being during this period. The enactment of the Korea Industrial Standards (1963) and Korean architectural and structural standards (1962) were accomplished during this period. The gymnasium was one of Korea's most significant technical challenges of the period.

7● Kyungdong Presbyterian Church

Kim Swoo-geun changed a lot in the wake of the controversy regarding his 1967 design of the Buyeo National Museum, which looked disturbingly similar to a Japanese Shinto shrine. In particular, he worked hard on reabsorbing Korean traditional architectural concepts and making them his own. Central to this was the concept of humanism—that architecture should focus on the user. Accordingly, buildings should be on an intimate, human scale. Like in a Korean home, space should naturally link the unit spaces within, and it should be multifunctional. Architecture should link inner and outer space, not artificially separate the two.

If Kim's earlier works were monumental structures that reflected Le Corbusier and Kenzo Tange, his later work were reflections of his own architectural world. **Kyungdong Presbyterian Church** is representative of this

stage in his career.

The church begins with an open plaza that connects with the main road, welcoming all. To the right is a long flight of steps that head to the entrance of the church, which is located in the back of the building. This path, called the Meditator's Walk, gives you a chance to prepare yourself for worship. This also provides a nice transitional space between the noisy outside world (this is Dongdaemun, after all) and the peaceful world of the chapel. The exterior is covered in unevenly broken red brick, an architectural expression of ecumenism—just as all the individual bricks form one mass, all are one within God. They also give the church a human, intimate feel.

The main tower, which some say looks like someone praying, symbolizes the prayer that the Kingdom of Heaven will one day present itself in the living world.

The interior, too, reflects the themes of ecumenism and community, and brings to mind a catacomb. Unfortunately for visitors, the church is open only for services, which are at 7:30pm on Wednesday and 10:00 and 11:30am on Sunday.

8❋ Gwanghuimun Gate

Along with Seosomun Gate (West Small Gate), **Gwanghuimun Gate** was one of the gates through which dead bodies were taken out of Seoul. It was built when Seoul's fortress walls went up in 1396, and rebuilt in 1422. In 1711, on the suggestion of scholar-official Min Jin-hu, it was rebuilt again by the capital garrison. The pavilion was built a bit later due to difficulty in procuring wood. In 1717, the pavilion was completed and a signboard with the name "Gwanghuimun" was hung. As part of the 1975 project to restore parts of the city walls, the stone gate was repaired and the wooden pavilion rebuilt.

9❋ Seo Gynecology Clinic

Korea's rapid development during the 60s and 70s emphasized function and utilitarianism, and the architectural "heritage" left behind from this period—row upon row of ugly concrete apartment blocks—still maligns the Seoul cityscape.

Nevertheless, there are jewels in the rough if you know

where to look. The **former Seo Gynecology Clinic** is one of them. Located just across the street from the Gwanghuimun Gate, this unique-looking building was designed in 1967 by Kim Chung-up, who is regarded along with Kim Swoo-geun as a pioneer of Korean architecture.

When we talk about Kim Chung-up, we're talking about Le Corbusier, the French architectural great who had a tremendous influence on Kim and his work. Kim spent four years in Le Corbusier's studio in France. In fact, Le Corbusier reportedly told Kim right before he returned to Korea that his homeland was too small for his talents.

The construction of the Seo Gynecology Clinic almost proved him right—Korea wasn't an easy place for a visionary architect in 1965, and lack of proper materials and limited local construction technology forced a very frustrated Kim to significantly alter his original design.

Still, what Kim eventually produced is a rather pretty piece of architecture with an obvious late Le Corbusier feel, as can be seen in the fluid curves and heavy walls of unadorned exposed concrete. The various sections of the building seem to flow together like an organic being. In the balconies, you can also see the influence of another architect Kim greatly admired, Antoni Gaudi.

Kim's most famous work is the French Embassy in Seoul. Another note about Kim—unlike Kim Swoo-geun, Kim Chung-up enjoyed very poor relations with Korean dictator Park Chung-hee, and he was virtually exiled to France in 1971. He worked in France and the United States until 1978, when he returned to Korea, where he remained until his death in 1988. Kim's poor relations with the Park Chung-hee administration are somewhat ironic, given that his mentor, Le Corbusier, apparently never met a dictator (regardless of ideology) he didn't like—when he wasn't pitching to Mussolini a new colonial capital for the recently conquered Ethiopia, he was submitting designs for the Palace of the Soviets, the great Stalinist monument in Moscow that never was.

10* Dongdaemun Stadium and Dongdaemun Design Plaza & Park

One apon a time—from 1925 to 2007, in fact—there used to be a grand sports complex just across from what is now Doosan Tower in Dongdaemun Market. Dongdaemun Stadium played an important role in the development of Korean sports, but the construction of newer sporting venues around the city decreased its utility. In 2007, Seoul City selected British female architect Zaha Hadid to take on Dongdaemun Design Plaza & Park, a landmark project of turning Dongdaemun Stadium into a park.

Her design, named "Motonymic Landscape," features a three-story (two above ground) Design Plaza and a park naturally connected in a wave design. The design, which begins at the Joseon-era city wall, attempts to provide flexibility of space through structures that bring to mind flowing water. The roof will feature a walking path with a grass field and a small lake, while Seoul's city walls will be left untouched in part of the park.

Work began on the park in May 2008, with completion scheduled for for first half of 2010. Construction is expected to cost around 227.4 billion won.

Archeological site at former Dongdaemun

11❋ The Bridges of Cheonggyecheon

The **Cheonggyecheon Stream** is a man-made stream filled with water originating from the mountains surrounding the capital such as Mt. Mongmyeonsan, Mt. Inwangsan, Mt. Bugaksan, and Mt. Naksan. It runs through Seoul from west to east for 11km before joining Jungnangcheon stream, which flows into the Hangang River.

There were many bridges over Cheonggyecheon such as Mojeongyo, Gwangtonggyo, Jangtonggyo, Supyogyo, Haranggyo, Hyogyeonggyo, Majeongyo, and Yeongdogyo, as well as floodgates such as Ogansumun.

Changes in the structures were made in line with the changes in the capital.

The remains of these bridges not only show the engineering technology of the Joseon era, but their installation and changes are also valuable materials in the study of the expanding function of the capital and the system for capital management.

❋ Gwangtonggyo Bridge Site

The **Gwangtonggyo Bridge** was the biggest bridge in Seoul. It was a central thoroughfare, linking the roads connecting Gyeongbokgung Palace, Yukjogeori, Jongno and Sungnyemun Gate, the major north-south route in the city. It was also surrounded by shops, making it the busiest bridge in Seoul. The bridge appears to have been built at the same time the city walls went up at the start of the Joseon era, although it was at first an earthen bridge. The stone version was built in 1410 on orders from King Taejong; it is said the bridge used stones from the tomb of Queen Sindeok, King Taejong's ill-loved stepmother.

❋ Ogansumun Floodgate Site

The **Ogansumun floodgate** was actually part of the Seoul Fortress wall. With five arched gates, the floodgate allowed the Cheonggyecheon Stream to flow out of the city. It is believed the gate was built when the Seoul Fortress walls

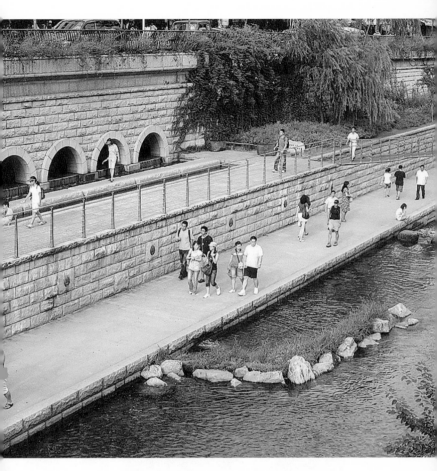

first went up, although this is uncertain. What is certain, however, is that in 1907, the gate was removed, ostensibly to allow the stream to flow smoother. The next year, the walls around Dongdaemun were removed as well.

Starting in the 1950s, Cheonggyecheon Steam was covered over with concrete. In 2003, however, Seoul Metropolitan Government began a project to restore the stream. As part of the project, the Ogansumun or at least a motif thereof was rebuilt.

12❀ Heunginjimun (Dongdaemun)

Heunginjimun, better known as Dongdaemun (Great East Gate), was the eastern entryway into the royal capital. Like Sungnyemun Gate (the pavilion of which was destroyed in a February 2008 fire), it was one of Seoul's four major gates. Also like Sungnyemun, it is located near a major market, the massive Dongdaemun Market.

Heunginjimun was first built at the time of the construction of the city walls in the late 14th century, although it would later undergo renovations. In 1869, however, it was completely rebuilt, the new structure somewhat larger than the original.

The gate is topped by a two-story pavilion that is five *kan* wide and four *kan* deep. The roof brackets are thin and highly decorated, typical of the latter Joseon era. The brackets supporting the roof are both on the columns and

between the columns. The gate also has a large semi-circular wall on the outside that was used to better protect the gate from enemies. Heunginjimun is the only one of Seoul's gates to have such a wall.

A Buddhist Community

TOUR *8
A Buddhist Community

Bongwonsa Temple

Bongwonsa is a rather unusual Buddhist temple. Unlike in most temples in Korea, the monks at Bongwonsa can marry, even if not every one does. They are members of the Taego Order, the second most important Buddhist order of Korea following the celibate Jogye Order. Accordingly, the temple is surrounded by a small village where the monks and their families reside.

Bongwonsa has a long and proud tradition of arts. In particular, it is famous for Buddhist painting and the Yeongsanjae, a traditional Buddhist ceremony combining music and dance.

❁ Taego Order of Korean Buddhism

The Taego Order of Korean Buddhism is one of some 27 Buddhist orders in Korea. Unlike the dominant Jogye Order, the Taego Order allows its monks to marry. This custom is a remnant of the Japanese occupation of Korea. Over 8,000 monks and 3,100 temples belong to this order. In fact, when Liberation came in 1945, there were more married monks than unmarried monks. When the Republic of Korea was established in 1948, the issue of clearing the vestiges of Japanese colonialism from Korean Buddhism became an issue, and in 1954, President Syngman Rhee decreed that married monks be thrown out of the temples, leading to a sharp divide between married and unmarried monks. In 1970, the married monks lost a lawsuit, which led to their separation from the Jogye Order to form the Taego Order.

The Taego Order is noted for its keeping of old Korean Buddhist traditions, including the color of its robes, its rituals and its practice of the Buddhist arts.

❁ A History of Korean Buddhism

Buddhism over the centuries has played a major role in the development of Korean culture.

Buddhism was first introduced to Korea in the fourth century AD. In 372, a Chinese monk entered the northern Korean kingdom of Goguryeo (37 BC–AD 668), bringing with him Buddhist texts and objects. The royal court in Goguryeo quickly adopted the new faith, making it the state religion.

In 384, a north Indian monk introduced Buddhism to Baekje (18 BC–AD 660), the kingdom that ruled the south-western part of the Korean Peninsula. As was the case in Goguryeo, he and his teachings were warmly received by the royal court, and Baekje became a strongly Buddhist nation.

In the southeastern kingdom of Silla (57 BC–AD 935), however, things were a bit different. Buddhism did not come to the relatively isolated Silla kingdom until the 5th

century. When it finally was introduced, via Goguryeo monks, it met with a warm reception from the Silla masses, but the aristocracy proved quite hostile to the foreign faith. In 527, a top court official announced that he'd become a Buddhist monk. The outraged court had him beheaded, but according to legend, when his head was severed, out poured not blood but milk. King Beopheung (r. 514–540), who was predisposed to Buddhist teachings anyway, used the miracle to remove barriers to Buddhism. His successor King Jinheung (r. 540–576) would make the faith the official one of the kingdom.

In 668, following a protracted struggle between Goguryeo, Baekje and Silla, the Silla kingdom finally succeeded in unifying the Korean Peninsula. In this age of stability and prosperity, Buddhism attained a golden age. Some of Korea's best known Buddhist treasures, including incredible Bulguksa Temple and Seokgulam Hermitage in Gyeongju, were built during this period. Some of Korea's greatest Buddhist monks, such as Wonhyo and Uisang, also lived at this time of great intellectual development. Buddhism also had a profound impact on the culture and arts of the Silla kingdom, as can be seen in the era's literature, architecture and sculpture.

Following a period of upheaval, the Silla kingdom collapsed, and was replaced by the Goryeo kingdom (918–1392). Like the Silla kingdom, the Goryeo kingdom adopted Buddhism as the state religion, and temples and monasteries grew large and powerful during this period. Unfortunately, the Buddhist establishment also grew corrupt through this wealth and power, leading to intense anti-Buddhist sentiment that would make itself all too apparent when the Goryeo Dynasty collapsed and was replaced by the strongly Confucian Joseon Dynasty.

The Goryeo Dynasty also witnessed the development of a school of Buddhist practice that would have a profound influence on Korean Buddhism, *Seon*. Better known in the West by its Japanese name, Zen, *Seon*—with its emphasis on meditation—first came to Korea in the latter part of the Unified Silla era. In the Goryeo era, it was at first viewed as a radical and dangerous challenge to the mainstream scholastics, but gradually over time, it earned widespread approval and state support. The 12th century Korean *Seon* monk Jinul, meanwhile, resolved the philosophical differences between the scholastic and *Seon* schools and founded one of the greatest of Korea's monasteries, Songgwangsa Temple.

One of the crowning achievements of Korean Buddhism —the production of the Tripitaka Koreana (a woodblock edition of the Buddhist scriptures)—was completed during the Goryeo era.

The collapse of the Goryeo Dynasty and the rise of the Joseon Dynasty witnessed a change in Buddhism's fortunes. The new regime promoted neo-Confucianism as its ruling ideology, and Buddhism—now associated with the corrupt *ancien régime*—was suppressed. Monks were chased from the cities into remote mountain areas, and strict controls were put on temples and their property.

The Japanese invasion of 1592, however, led to an improvement in the status of Korean Buddhism due to the widespread participation of Buddhist monks in the resistance to the Japanese invaders. Government control of the Buddhist religious establishment was still heavy (Buddhist monks were still banned from the cities, for example), but the government made no further attempts to stamp out the faith.

The occupation of Korea by Japan in 1910 created much turmoil for Korean Buddhism. Japan, like Korea, had a strong Buddhist tradition. Unfortunately, the colonial authorities promoted Japanese sects of Buddhism and interfered in Korea's traditional Buddhist practices. In particular, Korean Buddhist monks—who are traditionally celibate—were allowed to marry, as is the practice in Japan. This tore the Korean Buddhist community apart, leading to severe tensions following Korea's liberation from Japan in 1945. Korea's modernization and Westernization and the dramatic rise of Christianity in Korea would also impact Buddhism's place in Korean society.

Today, Korean Buddhism is one of Korea's largest religions. Half of Koreans who consider themselves religious identify themselves as Buddhists. Korean Buddhism's largest Buddhist sect is the Jogye Order, which was officially established in 1962, although its roots go back to the Goryeo era. Representative of post-Jinul Korean Buddhism, the Jogye Order blends both *seon* and scholastic Buddhism.

❁ Bongwonsa Temple

Bongwonsa Temple was founded by Grand Master Doseon (827–898) in 889, in the Unified Silla era. The temple was originally located in what is now the site of Yonsei University (also the site of Yeonhuigung in the 15th century). It was moved to its current location on a mountain near the university in 1748 by Master Chanjeup, with assistance from King Yongjo (r. 1725–1776). In fact, the original signboard for the temple was written by King Yongjo himself; the current signboard for the Judgment Hall was written by Jeong Dojeon, the great Confucian scholar.

Later, King Jeongjo (r. 1776–1800) would establish here the Chilgyu-Jeongso, a body to regulate clerical discipline and promote Buddhist society. The revolutionary monk Lee Dong-in—the spiritual mentor of Kim Ok-gyun, who led the Reformists' Coup of 1884—also spent five years here in the late 19th century, introducing Kim and his comrades to tales and images of the Western world.

The current temple compound took its shape in 1911, when it was reconstructed under the watch of then-abbot Lee Bo-dam. In 1945, the temple's monks built a large hall named the Yeombuldang to be used as an monument to Korean independence. This building was lost in a fire in September 1950; among the treasures lost was the original signboard written by Kim Yongjo and the remains of Kim Ok-hyun and Lee Dong-in. The hall was restored in 1966 when the Asojeong, a house that formerly belonged to the Regent of Korea, Prince Heungseon, was moved to the temple for use as a meeting hall for the monks.

In 1991, an accidental fire destroyed the Main Hall of the temple. In 1994, its reconstruction was completed, and shortly thereafter in the same year, the massive Samcheonbuljeon Hall (Hall of 3,000 Buddhas) was finished.

Bongwonsa is the head temple of the Taego Order of Korean Buddhism, and is particularly noted for its monks' contributions to Buddhist art. The late Yi Man-bong, a master of the Korean painting form of *dancheong*

(Important Intangible Cultural Property No. 48), resided here, as did Park Song-am, a master of the Buddhist musical rite of Yeongsanjae (Important Intangible Cultural Property No. 50).

❈ Buddhist Painting

Buddhist painting seeks to present the Buddhist world view and the teachings of the Buddha in visual form.

One form of Buddhist painting is the *taenghwa*, a Buddhist painting painted on silk or hemp. These paintings often show images of the Buddha and Bodhisattvas or depict the teachings of the Buddhist scriptures. The paintings are hung on the wall—often times, you will find these paintings behind the Buddha statue in the main hall of a temple.

Byeokhwa (murals), meanwhile, are Buddhist mural paintings painted directly on the wall. Traditionally, these paintings were painted on clay, wood and stone.

Kwaebul are huge Buddhist paintings that were hung outside during Buddhist rites. The most common image found on these paintings is the Buddha's Lotus sermon on Mt. Gridhrakuta (Vulture Peak, or in Chinese, Ling Jiu Shan).

Buddhist paintings can be drawn on cloth, paper, clay, wood, stone and metal. The most universal kind are done on cloth, particularly those found behind Buddha images and those used for outdoor ceremonies. Truth be told, there are very few old *kwaebul* still in existence; most are from the mid-to-late Joseon era. The oldest *kwaebul* in existence is the one at Jungnimsa Temple in Naju, Jeollanam-do, and was painted in 1623.

❀ Yeongsanjae Ceremony

The Yeongsanjae Preservation Association of Bongwonsa, which has preserved the tradition of the Yeongsanjae Ceremony (Important Intangible Cultural Property No. 50), holds regular performances of this most beautiful of Buddhist traditions for world peace and national reunification.

The Yeongsanjae Ceremony is a symbolic reenactment of the historical Buddha Sakyamuni's delivery of the Lotus Sutra on Mt. Gridhrakuta some 2,600 years ago, in which offerings are made to the Buddha and Bodhisattvas in attendance. The ceremony is held in hopes of leading both the living and the departed into the joy of enlightenment and perpetual peace.

Consequently, the Yeongsanjae Ceremony should be revered as a truly important Buddhist ritual, not as simply a 'performance." It is a ceremony that prays for the unity of the living and the deceased in the Dharma throughout

the universes, and it is Buddhism's most magnificent and impressive Buddhist ritual passed down through the ages.

❀ The S*P*I*C*E of Spirituality

By Brian Barry

Buddhist temple art serves the same purposes as religious art everywhere, namely to:

Sanctify * Protect * Inspire * Console * Educate

Although each temple is unique, most temples fit a basic pattern. The main hall on a compound is usually the "Hall of the Great Hero," or **Main Buddha Hall**. This is dedicated to the historical Buddha Sakyamuni and it sanctifies the grounds. Inside the Main Hall, there are usually three altars or "platforms."

* The **Main Platform** is at the center of the back wall. This usually includes major statues and a **Main Platform Painting** to support the statuary. The purposes of the statues and painting(s) are to sanctify the hall, to educate and to inspire.

* Usually on the right wall of the hall is a **Guardian Platform**. This includes an altar for incense and a **Guardian Painting.** The purpose is to protect the hall, the Buddhist teachings and Buddhist followers. The painting can educate and inspire as well as protect.

* Usually on the left side of the hall is a **Memorial Platform** for funeral and memorial services, and this may have any of a variety of paintings, including an **Ambrosia Painting**. This platform is to console the spirits of both the living and the departed. It can also be educational and inspirational.

In addition, most if not all buildings on a temple compound will feature **dancheong**, bright, decorative patterns on both the exterior and interior. These cosmic patterns allude to spiritual joy and paradise, and therefore are **inspirational**. In additional to being ornamental, "dancheong"seals out drafts and preserves the wood by repelling termites and other insects.

Murals on the outside of the halls and pavilions may include the "Eight Scenes from the Life of the Buddha" and other stories to teach about Buddhism in general or the temple in particular, and to inspire.

Bridge to the Contemporary

TOUR *9
Bridge to the Contemporary

Seoul Station to
Joongang Daily News Headquarters

Although now overshadowed by the skyscrapers and hustle-bustle that surrounds it, Seoul Station was at one time one of the most impressive buildings in Seoul. Designed to be a symbol of the power of the Japanese colonial authorities, Seoul Station dominated its surroundings and intimidated the viewer. Over the years, the station would develop into the transportation nexus of the nation and Seoul's major port of entry for people and goods. As more and more people flocked to Seoul during Korea's 20th century urbanization, the grand dome of Seoul Station was often the first thing they saw.

This walk will take us from Seoul Station to Yakhyeon Catholic Church (Korea's first Western-style Catholic church and an example of French missionary architecture) and the headquarters of one of Korea's major newspapers, the Joongang Daily News.

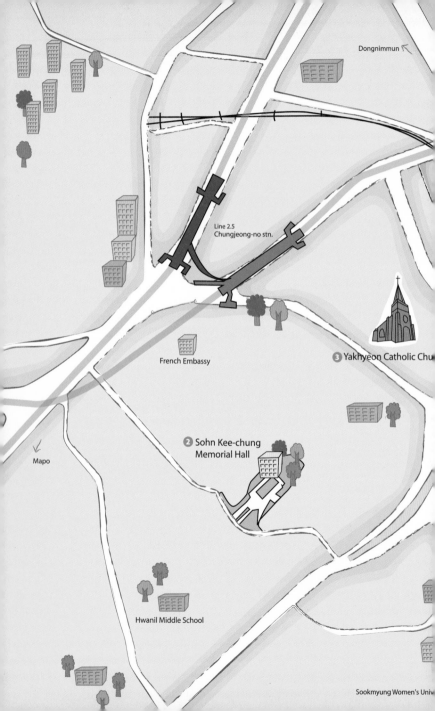

Dongnimmun

Line 2.5
Chungjeong-no stn.

French Embassy

❸ Yakhyeon Catholic Chu

❷ Sohn Kee-chung
Memorial Hall

Mapo

Hwanil Middle School

Sookmyung Women's Univ

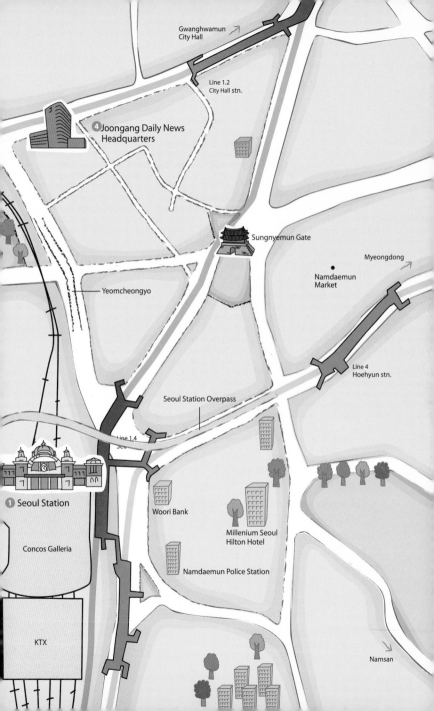

Gwanghwamun
City Hall

Line 1.2
City Hall stn.

4 Joongang Daily News
Headquarters

Sungnyemun Gate

Myeongdong

Namdaemun
Market

Yeomcheongyo

Line 4
Hoehyun stn.

Seoul Station Overpass

Line 1.4
Seo

1 Seoul Station

Woori Bank

Concos Galleria

Millenium Seoul
Hilton Hotel

Namdaemun Police Station

KTX

Namsan

1❋ Seoul Station

Old **Seoul Station** was one of the two major pieces of contemporary architecture from the Japanese occupation era, the other being the now departed Government-General Building.

Rail service came to Korea in 1899 with the opening of the 33km Noryangjin-Incheon line. With the opening of the Hangang Railway Bridge in 1900, Seoul proper was linked to Incheon, with Seoul's first station being Gyeongseong Station, built in Seodaemun, just west of Yeomcheongyo Bridge. In 1904, the Seoul-Busan line opened, and a new main terminal was built just south of the current one as Namdaemun Station, due to its proximity to Namdaemun. The Seoul-Sinuiju line opened in 1905, followed by the Seoul-Wonju line in 1914, creating the need for a new station. The growing war in China—and the need to ship troops and weapons to the front—added impetus to this, so in June 1922, work began on the grand Keijo (the Japanese name for Seoul) Station. Construction was completed in 1925.

Seoul Station was designed in Palladian fashion by Tokyo Imperial University professor Tsukamoto Yasushi, a student of Tatsuno Kingo, the man who designed Tokyo Station (and in Korea, the former headquarters of the Bank of Korea in Myeongdong). Seoul Station is supposedly modeled on Tokyo Station, which in turn is "rumored" to be modeled

on Amsterdam Central Station, making Seoul Station a copy of a copy. Regardless, it's a beautiful piece of Renaissance-style architecture.

The station is shaped like a square, with the main entrance in the middle. The center roof is crowned with a massive Byzantine dome, and makes for an impressive site. Four small towers were added later. The lower part of the structure is made of rusticated stone (like many Palladian structures), while the upper part is made of brick. Stone is used for the window frames and other decorations.

Another distinctly Palladian feature is the use of Diocletian windows. The Diocletian window is a semicircular window or opening divided into three compartments by two vertical mullions, and takes its name from the windows found in the Thermae (Baths) of Diocletian in Rome. Despite being of ancient Roman origin, the Diocletian window came back in fashion when Andrea

Palladio began using them in the 16th century. In Seoul
Station, the main hall is lit by a massive Diocletian window. Diocletian window are used on the upper parts of
the left and right annexes, too.

The roof is done up in natural slate, with bronze plating
used in places. In 1982–1983, the building underwent
restoration work and interior renovation.

The main waiting hall is a very impressive basilica-like
space. The stone for the pillars, coincidentally, was quar-
ried in Seoul.

Intended as a symbol of Imperial Japan's modernity and
sophistication, the station was luxuriously appointed,
down to the door handles and masonry on the stairwells.
It's all very evocative of the romance of the railroad of the
1920s. This is perhaps nowhere more apparent than the
old station restaurant on the second floor, complete with
chandeliers, a fireplace and Korea's first wall radiators.

The biggest problem facing old Seoul Station is that
nobody quite knows what to do with it. Originally, the
old station was supposed to be incorporated into the new

Seoul Station, but in the end, that didn't happen. Now, the station stands off to the side—"ostracized," if you will—serving no apparent purpose whatsoever. As a protected historic building, it's in no danger of being torn down, and work is being done to restore the interior, but no specific plans have been decided for its future use.

❋ Palladian Architecture

Palladian architecture is that based on the work of Italian architect Andrea Palladio (1508-1580), who is widely considered the most influential figure in the history of Western architecture. Particularly renowned for his designs of villas in the area around Venice, Palladio based his designs on the rationality and motifs of Roman architecture. During the 17th and 18th centuries, his work inspired architects all over Europe, with Palladian styles becoming particularly popular in England, Ireland and North America.

2❋ Sohn Kee-chung Memorial Park and Laurel Tree

There is a big tree in **Sohn Kee-chung Park**, formerly Yangjeong High School in Manni-dong. The tree, known as the Sohn Kee-chung laurel tree, has an interesting story. As legend would have it, the tree was a gift to Sohn from

German Chancellor Adolf Hitler—the laurel worn by Sohn during the medal ceremony was said to have been made from its leaves. Two trees were given—one was planted in Japan, and the other here. The one planted in Japan, however, supposedly dried up and died, while the one planted in Korea still thrives.

⁕ Sohn Kee-chung (1912–2002)

Born in Sinuiju, Pyonganbuk-do, Sohn Kee-chung was edu-
cated at Yangjeong High School and Meiji University in
Japan, from which he graduated in 1940. Between 1933
and 1936, he ran 13 marathons and won 10 of them. Sohn
became one of Korea's greatest sporting heroes when he
won the gold medal in the marathon in the 1936 Berlin
Olympics. Since Korea was then occupied by Japan, Sohn
unfortunately had to compete as a member of the Japanese
team. He reportedly cried when the Japanese flag was
raised and the Japanese national anthem played during the
medal ceremony. Japan was officially credited with Sohn's
gold in its 1936 Summer Olympic medal count.

Interestingly, the Dong-A Ilbo newspaper ran a photo of
Sohn at the awards ceremony, but edited the photograph to
remove the Japanese flag from his chest. This led the colonial authorities to arrest nine people connected with the
newspaper and to suspend its publication for nine months.

3⁕ Yakhyeon Catholic Church

Yakhyeon Catholic Church is extremely important in that it
was the first Western-style Catholic Church built in Korea.

Construction on the church began in 1891 and finished
the following year. The church was built just outside the
city walls, not far from where 44 Korean Catholics were
executed earlier in the century. Overseeing construction
was Father Eugene Coste of the Paris Foreign Missions
Society, who also designed Incheon's splendid Dapdong
Cathedral.

The church, which was completed six years ahead of
Myeongdong Cathedral, is not entirely Gothic—it's a mix-
ture of Gothic and Romanesque—but it's the Gothic part
that counts, as this would serve as as model for other
French-built churches in Korea (Gothic steeple, red and
black brick, etc.). In terms of Korean modern architecture, it's a rare example of pre-1900 Western architecture

that was taken directly from the West rather than through the Japanese.

The bricks, coincidentally, were baked in Korea, although the bricklaying itself was done by Chinese masons. When it was originally built, there was also an interior divider that separated the congregation into male and female sections in accordance with Korean social mores of the time. This partition was removed in 1921.

In 1998, much of the church was destroyed in a fire set by a drunk wayfarer. In 2000, the church was rededicated following a one year and six month restoration project.

❋ Catholicism in Korea

Unlike the Protestants, whose faith was introduced via
Western missionaries (who often doubled as educators,
diplomats and businessmen) who came to Korea legally in
the closing years of the 19th century, Catholicism came to
Korea much earlier, and as a result had a much rougher
time of it. After its introduction in the 18th century,
Catholicism was subject to several brutal persecutions—an
eight year persecution that began in 1866, for instance, led
to the deaths of some 8,000 Catholics. And Western
Catholic missionaries weren't immune—the 1866 persecution killed nine French priests.

To avoid the persecutions, Catholics fled into the mountains where they were relatively safe, forming villages (such
as the ones near Wonju) where they made a living farming
or making earthenware jars. In this regard, their experience
was not entirely dissimilar from that of the Buddhists—
during the early Joseon era, Buddhists were virtually forced
from the cities and into the mountains, and their faith subject to severe restrictions. Even though, by the time
Catholicism entered the scene, official persecution of
Buddhism had eased considerably, the Buddhists could at

least empathize with the Catholic' plight.

Interestingly, Catholicism was introduced to Korea *sans* not only missionaries, but also any real effort to bring the faith to the country. From the Catholic Encyclopedia:

> *"[I]n a manner perhaps unique in the annals of the Church, the Faith was introduced there [Korea] without preaching and before any missionaries had penetrated the country. The educated people, more eager for new knowledge the more their country was jealously closed, procured through the annual embassy to Peking all the books possible upon science, literature, etc. Some Christian books fell into their hands, and, the grace of God aiding, they recognized the truth. One of them, Ni-seung-houn, undertook in 1784 the journey to Peking and was baptized there, under the name of Peter. Upon his return he baptized his companions, who, like himself, were men of learning and high position. That their faith was firm, events proved. In 1791 Paul Youn and Jacques Kouen sealed their belief with their blood for having refused to offer sacrifice upon the occasion of the death of their relatives. Connected by reason of its origin with the Church of Peking, Corea was dependent upon that vicariate until 1831. About the year 1794, a Chinese priest, Father Jacques Tjyou, was sent to Corea. Upon his arrival he found about 4000 faithful. After seven years of a heroic and fruitful ministry he was arrested and put to death, 31 May, 1801."*

One of the early converts to the faith was renowned *sil-hak* ("Practical Learning," a school of Confucian thought emphasizing social reform and scientific learning) scholar Dasan Jeong Yag-yong, whose list of accomplishment includes the design of Suwon Hwaseong Fortress.

The French—and the Society of Foreign Missions of Paris in particular—began coming to Korea in the early 19th century, albeit clandestinely. In a political environment hostile to Catholicism and the presence of foreign missionaries, one mistake could doom the entire community. Three French missionaries were beheaded in one persecution in 1839. In 1845, a new French bishop arrived, bringing with him a young missionary and Korea's priest, the Macao-trained Andrew Kim. Kim was captured and executed the following year.

Only in the late 19th century, with the signing of diplomatic relations with the imperial powers of the West, did conditions improve for Korean Catholics. French missionary priests were granted the right to operate openly, and churches and seminaries were built throughout the country. After Japan annexed Korea in 1910, however, things grew difficult for Korean Catholics as churches and missionaries were harassed.

Today, Catholicism is one of the most prominent religions in Korea. During the 1980s, it played an important role in Korea's democratization struggle by sheltering pro-democracy dissidents from the authorities. The beautiful Myeongdong Cathedral in downtown Seoul was particularly famous as a place of refuge for political dissidents during the turbulent period.

4✷ Joongang Daily News Headquarters and Korea Foundation Cultural Center

The headquarters of **Joongang Daily News** was big news when it was built in the 1980s, utilizing new construction techniques not yet seen in Korea.

The project, part of a Seoul City scheme at the time to redevelop the Seosomun area, mixes rounded and straight corners to break away from the "boxy" styles of the day and project the upright image befitting a media company.

The building uses red granite with a slippery and balanced feel. The building is divided into three parts—offices, the newspaper company and a theater and gallery.

The building's entryways make use of the inclined ground to allow easy access from all directions. The building also emphasizes its public nature with outside sculpture gardens and a rooftop garden.

The building is home to the Hoam Gallery and Hoam Art Hall. The Hoam Gallery is being used as the **Korea Foundation Cultural Center**.

In late June 2005, the Korea Foundation opened the Korea Foundation Cultural Center in the Hoam Gallery to allow foreigners residing in Korea a place to understand and experience Korean and world culture. The first floor has an exhibit room and a library, while the second floor has a seminar room and a small theater.

✳ Cho In-souk

A master architect, president of Daaree Architect & Associates and noted expert on Korean traditional architecture, Cho has been active not only in the preservation of Seoul's increasingly precious architectural heritage, but also sharing that heritage with Seoul's Korean and foreign communities through the Seoul Foundation for Arts & Culture's "Culture is My Friend" program. Her work is characterized by the drive to integrate Korean traditional architectural principles into Korea's modern architecture. Cho also lectures on Korean Buddhist architecture for the International Dharma Instructors Association and sat on Seoul Metropolitan Government's Hanok Conservation Committee (2001–2009 April) and the Evaluation Committee of the Cultural Properties Administration.

✳ Robert Koehler

A resident of Korea for over a decade, Robert is the editor-in-chief of SEOUL, a monthly culture and travel magazine co-published by Seoul Selection and Seoul Metropolitan Government. He also co-led the Seoul Foundation for Arts & Culture's "Culture is My Friend" program in 2007.

When he isn't working on SEOUL, he's either blogging (www.rjkoehler.com) or traveling throughout Korea, taking photos of old buildings.